Multipreneurship

Multipreneurship

Diversification in Times of Crisis

NICHOLAS HARKIOLAKIS

Routledge
Taylor & Francis Group

LONDON AND NEW YORK

First published 2014 by Gower Publishing

2 Park Square, Milton Park, Abingdon, Oxfordshire OX14 4RN
52 Vanderbilt Avenue, New York, NY 10017

Routledge is an imprint of the Taylor & Francis Group, an informa business

First issued in paperback 2020

Gower Applied Business Research
Our programme provides leaders, practitioners, scholars and researchers with thought provoking, cutting edge books that combine conceptual insights, interdisciplinary rigour and practical relevance in key areas of business and management.

British Library Cataloguing in Publication Data
A catalogue record for this book is available from the British Library

Library of Congress Cataloging-in-Publication Data
Harkiolakis, Nicholas.
 Multipreneurship : diversification in times of crisis / by Nicholas Harkiolakis.
   pages cm
 Includes bibliographical references and index.
 ISBN 978-1-4724-1103-7 (hardback) -- ISBN 978-1-4724-1104-4 (ebook) --
 ISBN 978-1-4724-1105-1 (epub) 1. Diversification in industry. 2. Entrepreneurship. I. Title.
 HD2756.H367 2014
 658.5'038--dc23

                                                                    2014000120

 ISBN 13: 978-1-4724-1103-7 (hbk)
 ISBN 13: 978-0-367-67006-1 (pbk)

Contents

List of Figures

About the Author

Nicholas Harkiolakis is Senior Vice President, Executive Coaching Consultants, in Athens, Greece, and leads negotiations between the European Commission and Technology consortia he represents. Dr. Harkiolakis has 25 years' experience as a technology educator and practitioner. He has served as a project manager on information technology projects and taught IT and research methods to undergraduate and graduate business students. He is currently a Research Fellow at Brunel University Business School in the UK. He teaches e-negotiations at the Normandy School of Business in France and his research interests embrace social networks mining and analysis, e-business and e-commerce, IT management and strategy, business intelligence, and optimization. Dr. Harkiolakis has authored or co-authored several books, including *e-Negotiations* for Gower.

Chapter 1
Introducing Multipreneurship

Economic activity of any form is initiated when people begin to interact and exchange interests and values. Gain of any form can be considered economic although the term is reserved for monetary or equivalent rewards. It's easy to see how even investments of a social nature, such as having a friend, can result in economic gains even if those are not expressed in monetary terms. A friendship, for example, fills certain aspects of our life such as the need to share. Leaving that need unexpressed and boiling inside can be at the expense of valuable awareness and attention that otherwise could easily be directed in investments with economic returns. By placing utility in almost everything, even in a rough form, one can convert a whole life into an economic theory that, although uninspired, could very well explain many facets of our social engagements.

The reason the presentation of this book's material started in such a pragmatic and materialistic fashion is simply to ease the introduction of the topic in a way that could relate to anyone interested in some way or another. Entrepreneurship in its most generic form is probably the foremost economic activity that humans engage in and the root of the progress and advancement we have achieved up to now. But how can we define the phenomenon in a way that allows for meaningful observation and the deduction of reliable conclusions? There is the classical historical approach of its appearance on scientists' radar, as well as an account of the phenomenon from a sociological perspective, especially since economic activities in the form of trade and money exchange pre-existed a scientific approach to study them.

In this book, while we will present both, we will root our analysis in a modern perspective as it's seen and understood by the people that engage in entrepreneurial activities. This behavioral approach will help answer the questions of: Who the entrepreneurs are? How did they evolve to become multipreneurs and why do they act? The focus will be on personality traits and the structure of the environment that allowed these traits to mature and flourish.

A major argument in the published literature is that entrepreneurs happened to be at the right time and place, with the right qualifications and the ability to see and take advantage of an opportunity that appeared in the market. While this stance makes absolute sense, the position of this book is that these attributes mostly affect the magnitude and extent of the entrepreneurial venture and do not influence its appearance. The same way that most seeds will grow to be tall and healthy trees in fertile and sunny ground, some seeds would also grow in a harsh environment only to become now smaller trees. In the eyes of the nurture or nature dilemma, the stance of this book is that nature will prevail even in harsh environmental conditions. By saying that we don't mean that entrepreneurship cannot be taught and cultivated. It simply states that in a properly "nourished" and susceptive environment, we can grow a forest of trees of different sizes, while in a harsh environment only the strongest of them will survive. In that sense proper policies and government support can turn an economy into a forest of entrepreneurial ventures, while luck of support can turn it into a desert.

To make this more apparent let's consider the case of an existing multipreneur, Richard Branson. According to our stance here, Branson would have expressed the entrepreneurial attitudes and become successful even if he was born in an isolated mountain village in Tibet. Sure, his empire wouldn't be as global as it is now, but for sure he would've been the Tibetan Richard Branson of his village. Although this proposal might sound arbitrary and absolute, it is hoped that by the end of the book it will have adequate support to trigger enough reaction to support or reject it by fellow academics. One contributes to knowledge even by rejecting a hypothesis as long as the tools used in the process conform to scientific practices and the logic of our era.

Focusing on the extreme case of multipreneurship in this book is meant to highlight the absolute minimum of the drives and personality traits that persist in all cases, whether hidden from the consciousness of the entrepreneurs or visible in broad daylight. The approach followed is similar to learning about the weather by studying a hurricane. Extremes can provide the essence of a phenomenon that in normal conditions can be obscured by the "noise" of other unrelated variables. Following the analogy of the weather phenomenon, a breeze can be influenced by local variables such as the morphology of the terrain (valleys, forests, water bodies, etc.) that could hide the underlying causes such as temperature differences and the rotation of the earth that can be prevalent in the formation of a hurricane and are generally accepted as vital constituents of any weather phenomenon.

Coming to the issue of entrepreneurship, there might be inherent variables such as, for example, boredom that can be at the core of entrepreneurship and would normally be hidden in normal entrepreneurs under the disguise of needs such as employment, independence, control, influence, etc. In multipreneurs, though, we might find that this variable is the main driving force beyond any control issues or insecurities about the future that one would normally consider as a driver for multipreneurs. Additionally, by studying multipreneurs we minimize the influence of the time and place of the opportunities entrepreneurs realize, since we will impose the element of diversity in the ventures. It is unlikely that the specific experience one gains from a certain market segment will be of significant value in comparison with a different one, so in that sense we ensure that the behavioral characteristics of the individual are at the core of their motivation and success.

Studying and presenting multipreneurship can be also quite frustrating, as most subjects that deal with expressions of human intelligence, but it can also be stimulating and revealing as it unfolds the practices and potential of the human intellect. Although commonalities between the various definitions of entrepreneurship and subsequently multipreneurship do exist, a definition can only be approached after an agreement of its constituent elements and their relationships is uniquely identified and described. Given the stage of the research in the field, an attempt will be made to establish a definition that can be a guide for the rest of the material in the book and one that will form the basis of further discussion.

Entrepreneurship will be attributed to any activity that leads to the accumulation of wealth beyond the vital needs for survival of an individual. In that sense an entrepreneur is more like a voracious beast always seeking new opportunities and ways to expand his visibility and sphere of influence. It was that thirst for control and recognition that moved ancient explorers to discover new places, conquerors to occupy new territory and merchants and traders to exchange goods and services for profit. While this approach might sound less romantic than some of the ways modern theorists try to approach entrepreneurship, it does more justice to the extreme case of multipreneurs that is the subject of this book.

For all purposes in this book entrepreneurship is considered any activity that explores economic opportunity (or the creation of wealth in other terms) through the creation and management of a business in the form of a sole proprietor, a partnership or the formation of a corporation. Based on that, *multipreneurship will be viewed as the initiation and the creation by an individual of more than one distinct and diverse business that reached maturity and coexisted for some period of time under his management and control.* While a lot of ventures will start as corporations, the last requirement is meant to indicate that the involvement of the entrepreneur is absolutely essential for the existence and function of the business. This distinction eliminates from our definition venture capitalists and investors who, while they might own a venture, they delegate its management to someone else. The definition also makes sure that the amount of time the parallel activities need to coexist should at least be enough for them to acquire maturity. This requirement is important and will exclude many categories of entrepreneurs such as serial/habitual entrepreneurs. Venture capitalists are also excluded from the definition unless they are considerably involved in the management of at least two of the businesses they support that are also diverse enough to belong to different industries. Further analysis of the typology of entrepreneurs will be made in the following chapter, so for the time being the definition stated above will serve as reference for the rest of the book.

Although our definition of a multipreneur implies both entrepreneurial and managerial qualities, the distinction of the two functions needs to be emphasized here. Clearly managerial skill and function are components of the multipreneur according to our definition above. Unlike the manager's function, though, a multipreneur is the primary owner of the uncertainty arising from the operation and establishment of the ventures they are involved in. This is a vital and fundamental difference as it impacts their engagement and commitment to the survival and success of their business a lot more than that of a manager. The ownership stake of the entrepreneur/owner is much higher than that of a manager, so when these roles are separated one does not expect a manager to express the same entrepreneurial mindset as that of the owner.

Typical stages that we observe in almost all self-made entrepreneurs (Figure 1.1) include beginning as a specialist practicing a profession according to some skills and traits (blue circle in Figure 1.1) he inherited and acquired through education and training. At this stage the individual is probably self-employed (solo entrepreneur) or employed under another entrepreneur or business. We will consider this the stage of *incubation* since the full display of entrepreneurial behavior is under development. When the build-up of entrepreneurial potential reaches a threshold (specific to each entrepreneur and to the environment they operate in), the individual ventures into forming his own business. At this stage he delegates specialty skills to others and his role becomes that of a generalist who coordinates and oversees the activities of

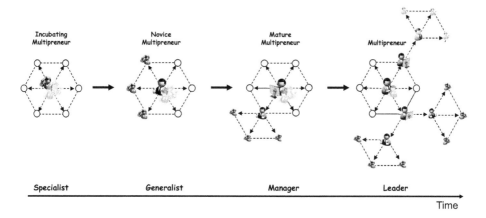

Figure 1.1   Evolution of an entrepreneur in time

his employees while occasionally performing specialty skill-related work. This is the earliest display of entrepreneurial behavior and we consider him now as a *novice* entrepreneur. As the business grows and more people get involved in the business, a divisional structure will begin to emerge from the entrepreneur/ owner's need to manage his expanded workforce and business operations. He is now a mature entrepreneur quite familiar with all aspects of his business operations and comfortable with coordinating and supervising his workforce. At this stage he is managing people more than anything else and we consider him now to be a *mature* entrepreneur. This is usually the highest stage most entrepreneurs reach in their lives.

As often happens, though, with most human activities, talent occasionally exists in surplus, so in the case of certain mature entrepreneurs we observe their evolution to an elevated stage where they are growing and replicating their businesses in different locations. Higher-profile entrepreneurs will expand their reach across continents, while others will limit their expansion within their national borders. In both cases the entrepreneurs have built a *portfolio* of businesses and their involvement now is concerned with leading the management teams of their business entities. They have now become true leaders, leaving the management and day-to-day running to their delegates and intervening only in exceptional circumstances.

If we turn Figure 1.1 counterclockwise by 90 degrees (Figure 1.2), it would resemble the sprouting of entrepreneurship and the flowering of the entrepreneurial tree. The ground here represents the place where the majority of people work, either self-employed or in other businesses. As we said before, if the soil is fertile with minerals and the seed is healthy, all we will need is water and sunshine and it will sprout and grow. Sometimes the seed will carry with it the ingredient to produce different flowers in the same tree (right image on Figure 1.2). This will show at the later stage when the experienced entrepreneurs decide to diversify and become multipreneurs.

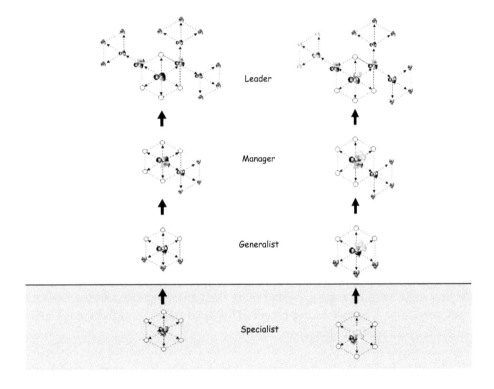

Figure 1.2   Entrepreneurial and multipreneurial growth

1.1   The Creation Process

The steps required for the development of an entrepreneur have been extensively analyzed and presented in numerous research publications and, in summary, we can say they involve: opportunity identification; outsourcing of resources for the formation of the business; and exploitation of the opportunity. Entrepreneurs are members of their societies and the world at large and in that perspective they live and interact with individuals, organizations and the market. If we could visualize (Figure 1.3) the world of the business as composed of different entities that include people, resources and opportunities, we can form a network of nodes

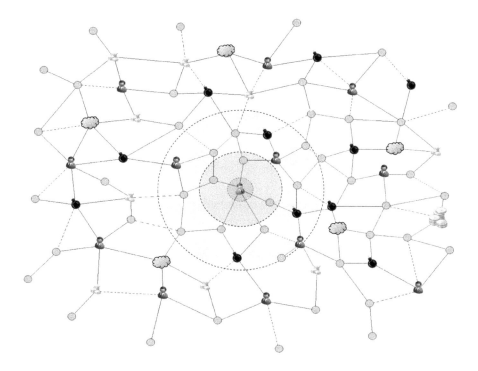

Figure 1.3   Business world from the perspective of the entrepreneur

and connections that at each instance of time can represent the position and status of an individual in relation to this abstract world/market representation.

Some of the nodes could represent personal attributes such as intelligence, courage, persistence, will and drive, while others could represent resources that entrepreneurs can utilize such as money, experience and their network of family members, friends, professional acquaintances and even organizations. To classify the environment, consenting regions around the entrepreneur are used as an approximation of his internal and inherent characteristics and values (light blue circle—no internal structure is shown due to limited size), his close family and friends circle he regularly interacts with (pink circle) and his expanded network of acquaintances and resources he has established in his life up to that point (yellowish circle). Outside these regions lies the vastly unexplored region of world resources and connections that to some extent can be visible to the entrepreneur but not reached yet.

In this representation, success (gold in our image) and failure (black bombs) are also included as nodes in the entrepreneurial space. Obviously one could add many more different types of symbols and connectors that could represent every possible aspect and entity that might exist in the world of an entrepreneur, but for the purposes of the analysis here the elements chosen are adequate for now. Connections between nodes will be used to easily display influence and dependencies either formed (solid lines) or in progress/potential (dotted lines) and will in general form the sphere of influence of the individual. Again, different attributes of the lines (such as thickness and color) could be used to represent finer classifications for the connectors, but for our simplified version used here the adopted ones will suffice.

The extent of the entrepreneur's influence network can be seen as the space within the possible networks that connect every actively engaged individual and resource of the business world we live in, that is or could be influenced physically and conceptually by the individual entrepreneur. Conceptually is meant to indicate here that nodes can be created or removed dynamically as the entrepreneur formulates ideas and relationships between other entities and resources. An alternative visual representation would be to think of it as a wetland that one attempts to cross by throwing stepping stones in the water to form pathways to dry spots until he reaches his destination. In that type of representation an opportunity is any path that connects the entrepreneur to success, which is nothing other than wealth-creation according to the definition adopted in this book. Apparently there can be many or no opportunities based on the availability of paths, but intuitively we can see that the denser the network, the stronger the possibility of paths that could lead to success. In fact, the denser network would most likely ensure multiple opportunities available and within the reach of the entrepreneur.

Let's assume for all purposes that Figure 1.4 depicts the identification of an opportunity by an entrepreneur outside his spheres of influence. Having spotted the opportunity, the entrepreneur now begins to visualize possible pathways (or stepping stones) he might follow to reach it. Visualizing a solid destination route (red arrows in Figure 1.5) is vital for success as the wrong paths (blue arrows in Figure 1.5) could lead to dead ends or, even worse, failure. In fact, there could be more than one path to reach the destination, but eventually the entrepreneur will decide on the one that appears more efficient, in terms of the resources it involves, the people it connects and the distance it covers.

Identifying the stepping stones should be seen as a dynamic process that evolves in time. At each stepping stone the entrepreneur would have to visualize potential pathways to the remaining route and choose the optimum ones he

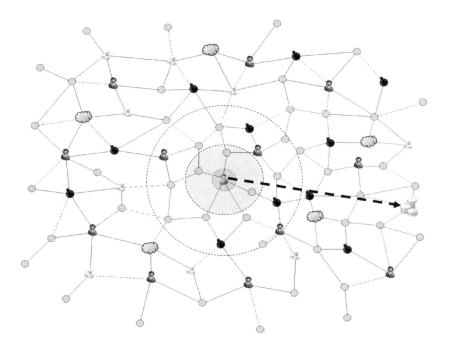

Figure 1.4   Opportunity identification

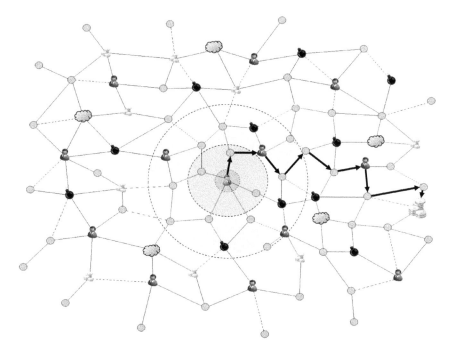

Figure 1.5   Pathway to success

believes will get him to his destination. Often he will need to backtrack and follow alternative routes, while at other times he might even need to build new stepping stones to reach his destination. Eventually one of these pathways will appeal to him for some reason or another and will become his choice of action.

This is where things get interesting, as the entrepreneur in essence solves problems along the way, exploring the space around him and establishing shortcuts (Figure 1.6) that will get him to the opportunity faster and more efficiently. This is the actual process of building his organization until finally he has developed a profitable product or service. Eventually a direct link to success (Figure 1.7) is established. At that time the creation process is complete and will give way to managing the entities that comprise the venture and streamlining its operations.

While the situation of Figure 1.7 establishes a successful entrepreneur, it is the process that proves entrepreneurial attitudes and, as such, there will at times be failures while at other times ideas will just stay as a concept on the drawing board. In fact, one could say that for most people it will remain just a

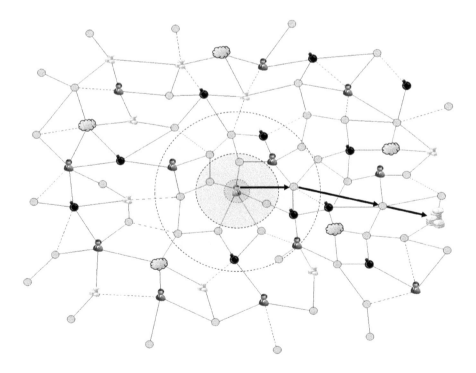

Figure 1.6   **Building shortcuts to success**

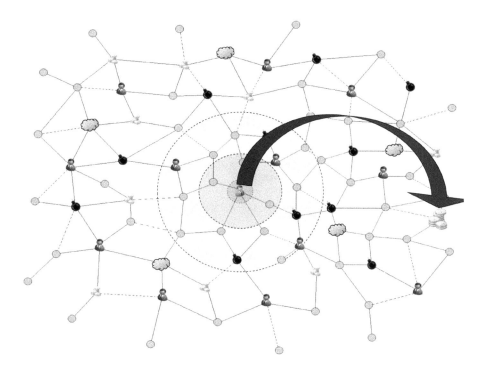

Figure 1.7   Maturing into success

dream that formed at some time or another and didn't manage to materialize. It could be lack of strong vision, resources (both physical and spiritual) or even an adequate extended network that could provide a pathway to success. Regardless of the reasons, failures will be there. But for the successful entrepreneur these will be more like opportunities for learning than irreversible obstacles in the way of his passion for success.

Figure 1.8 shows a more realistic situation, especially in the case of mature multipreneurs, as it depicts their ventures that lead to success and others that lead to failures or dead ends. To make it more realistic, some of the nodes have been replaced with "clouds" to represent situations where the entrepreneur cannot see or fully understand where a connection leads. The online dimension that the Internet revolutions created can be expressed as such. An even more precise representation would have some nodes as enforcing or inhibiting the entrepreneurial attitudes. Hopefully as the presentation of the topic and the analysis of the various cases progress, these details will be more prevalent and allow us at the end to draw solid conclusions and build a realistic model of the phenomenon.

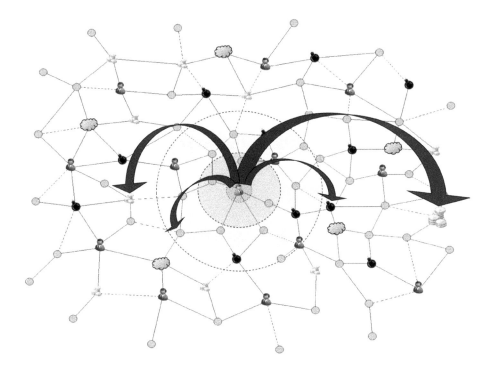

Figure 1.8   Multipreneurial growth

1.2   The Book Structure

Limitations of all sorts can influence the structure, contents and the truths a book is trying to uncover. Given the vastness of the entrepreneurship field and the limited size of this book, we have attempted to give a complete and detailed coverage of the phenomenon of multipreneurship from an academic point of view but rather an informal but critical account of all aspects involved in its expression. A choice was also made to avoid the presentation of failures (opposites in a sense) that could otherwise strengthen and validate the deductions we will make about the positives. Multipreneurship is an island in a sea of entrepreneurship and would be extremely difficult to identify accurately clear cases of unsuccessful attempts at the same level of public awareness as the successes. The primary goal of this book is to intrigue the reader and contribute with a fresh eye (hopefully) to the science and the evolution of business practices that can benefit individuals and societies. In that respect it can be considered as a merge between an academic and a lay reader's book that introduces the phenomenon and offers possible explanations for practitioners and theorists to consider and test.

A general consensus made in this book is the terminology adopted regarding entrepreneurship and multipreneurship and the way references to one also imply the other. Multipreneurship is by default inclusive of entrepreneurship, so any reference to the latter also includes the former but not the other way round. Although we will clarify this further when we present the respective typology, it is good to keep in mind the distinction as occasionally the use if the entrepreneurship/entrepreneur is used to also reflect multipreneurship/multipreneur. Another case that might draw criticism is the use of "he" when talking about multipreneurs. With apologies to the female readers this is not meant to discriminate but rather to reflect the realities of the subject as it is by itself gender-biased.

The following chapters are organized in categories where different expressions of the phenomenon will be presented. To give the reader a heads-up on the status of the research and our understanding up to now, a review of the academic attempts and the frameworks developed will be presented in Chapter 2. For the lay reader these aspects might not be of interest, so skipping that chapter will not influence the understanding of concepts presented later. It will, though, provide a valuable account of how theorists see and try to make sense of social phenomena. This type of knowledge is valuable as it forms the basis upon which policy recommendations are made and stronger concepts are built that further highlight the hidden aspects of multipreneurship.

After the review of the existing theoretical frameworks, we start with the presentation of the expression of multipreneurship at the micro level first and then the macro levels. At the micro level (Chapter 3) we look at low-level multipreneurship as a way of survival in societies and cultures that are exposed to high volatility and uncertainty. These multipreneurial activities are usually localized with limited reach and rarely expand beyond national borders. At the macro level of high-profile multipreneurs (Chapter 4) we will see individuals that build successful and diverse international organizations strong enough to survive and succeed globally. Obviously the number of the latter cases is much smaller than the former, so at the macro level we will see in more detail specific individuals who made their mark in the global arena and who, to a great extent, act as role models for future multipreneurs. Both Chapters 3 and 4 will also cover cultural aspects that influence the appearance of multipreneurship.

Chapter 5 will take us away from the individuals and to organizations that exhibit multipreneurship tendencies. Classical examples are conglomerates that include diverse organizations in their portfolios. Although in such cases it will be difficult to attribute personal characteristics to the management team of a conglomerate, we will be able to identify the factors that led to the formation of these entities and the spirit that influenced their evolution and growth.

In Chapter 6 we will bring everything together in the form of a framework. This hopefully will explain a lot of the characteristics of the phenomenon in a more coherent and easily understood way that could form the basis for further improvements and understanding of the issues involved. The ultimate goals of such an endeavor/framework will always be its ability to make as accurate as possible predictions for the potential of people and organizations to act as multipreneurs. Prospective multipreneurs should have by now a good understanding of what multipreneurship is and the drives behind entrepreneurs that help them transcend into venturing and controlling multiple and diverse ventures.

The book closes with a chapter on scaling the phenomenon of mulitpreneurship as a means for economic growth. Different aspects that do not dominate the field, such as female and social multipreneurship, the new medium that the Internet introduced and educational attempts to multiply the supply of multipreneurs, will be discussed. The chapter also attempts to bring our findings to the policy-making level so governments and public institutions help them formulate strategies and take actions that would allow the scaling-up of multipreneurship. Such efforts will ensure economic growth as multiplication of entrepreneurial activity by capable and already successful entrepreneurs will serve as an asset for exploitation.

In closing it is my intention to transmit and share some of the fascination for the subject of multipreneurship and those visionary multipreneurs that crossed the boundaries of single ventures and became the heroes of the business world as we know it today. Like hurricanes, these individuals swiped the markets, bringing fresh opportunities into existence and creating ventures that leave their mark on their local economies and the world at large.

Chapter 2
Theoretical Perspectives

The importance of entrepreneurs in economic growth became evident to theorists early on in modern times, so one can now find numerous theoretical approaches to entrepreneurship that try to explain the origins of the phenomenon and its expressions and impact in societies and economies. Along with finding out why entrepreneurs exist, the process by which they create and control their business becomes critical as it will help governments and policy-makers provide support for such initiatives. While a lot of progress has been made in researching entrepreneurship and we now have many empirical studies that report success (although limited and ambiguous) in explaining entrepreneurial behavior and processes, there are still pending issues that prevent the formulation of a comprehensive description.

Challenges include the incorporation of critical contributors such as opportunity identification, persistence, imagination, creativity and the ability to exploit the potential of resources and networks. As theories were advancing it became evident that entrepreneurship is by itself a complex phenomenon and as such it requires sizable models to allow representation of its many features. A theory needs to account for the influences of the entrepreneur's environment, such as competition from other firms, partnerships, alliances, regulatory bodies and the consumer, with all its complexity (location, reach, behavior, etc.). The greater and more sophisticated the skills of those players, the more complex the environment, making a theoretical analysis and representation more demanding.

Entrepreneurs express their higher needs for independence and control of their own destiny through financial initiatives that lead to firm formation. Nowadays, they are perceived as people who create businesses and open up the way for new industries to emerge, precipitating in this way to structural changes in the economy and commercializing new products and services. They are not to be confused with financers or venture capitalists (although the one does not exclude the other) since they rely heavily on financial support from outside sources. Although they usually commit their private financial resources, their primary contribution to their business is in the form of human and network resources. Profit is a motivating factor but as we saw before and will become evident later on, especially in the case of multipreneurs, there are other higher needs behind their drives and accomplishments.

2.1   Crash Intro to Economics

Economists like to make the distinction between needs and wants clear as it helps in forming equations they can process and from which they can derive conclusions. Of course the state of our economies is a testimony to their difficulties in representing them and the long way we have to go to find a realistic model of the economy. In that perspective our humble attempt here is only meant to introduce basic characteristics that will be necessary later on for the understanding of multipreneurship. Probably the most important economic term we will need in our attempt to provide a theory of entrepreneurship and, later, multipreneurship is that of the *market*.

The accessible universe that resources and needs form is traditionally called "the market". This is like the physical environment but in a more abstract form and can include physical resources as well as products and services created by humans and available to everyone with access to the market. Traditional economists view the market as a black box, where a kind of a "magical" process—competition—moves things around until a balance is achieved between prices and quantities (Richardson 1960). Entrepreneurs are almost invisible in that perspective and the supply and demand are the forces that give life to the market. This is not a bad perspective as we do the same (at least the theorists amongst us) with the physical world, when we try to explain it and predict its function in terms of science, instead of passively accepting a God-like creator and controller. Our evolution and achievements stand as testament to that.

A critical aspect of a market is that at any single moment in time, only a fixed amount of resources are available. This creates a situation known as *scarcity*, which in simple terms means that people (some or many) cannot afford to satisfy their needs (higher order mainly) by having the appropriate offering (such as money or labor). This is not to be confused with *shortages* as the latter implies destruction of limited supply of goods and services due to disasters (natural, such as hurricanes or floods, or manmade, such as wars, over-farming and over-mining). Scarcities should be seen as steady elements in markets because of competing alternative uses for resources. Land, capital and labor, for example, could become scarcities due to growth in certain fields and territories over others.

Similarly, entrepreneurship could become a scarcity simply because it affects the production of goods and services. Nowadays, technology also tends to be considered a scarcity because it affects the use of land and labor to develop, manufacture and distribute products and services more efficiently.

The trade-offs of goods and services form the *economic activity* that our modern societies are engaged in. Typical exchanges involve sacrificing income to buy a good, such as a laptop or a mobile. Exchanges take place in time and space and in that respect one chooses to invest their time and space in one activity over another, making the single next best alternative to the chosen one the *opportunity cost*. This is like the difference in value we place between activities. Provided our current choice is more valuable than the second best alternative, one would be better off considering choice as gains over the alternative, instead of as opportunity cost simply because cost is mainly associated with expense or loss.

The way resources are used to address needs is called an *economic system*. In such systems the major questions are what, how and for whom to produce. The answers we give form the variety of economic systems we have today and they range from traditional (based on historic family trade), controlled (such as communism and its variations), capitalist and combinations of all of them. Given that our research subject is multipreneurship, the focus here will be on capitalist or pure market economies that allow any individual to engage in entrepreneurial ventures. Economists like free markets because they can deliver maximum economic wealth with minimum administration. In such systems governments act primarily as regulators, leaving economic decisions to the individuals, who by nature will be looking after the interests and welfare of their own. Individuals are in control of how and what they will produce and benefit from the income received from selling their labor and resources. These choices are not necessarily guided by tradition, as was the case in the past, but by their knowledge of the market structure.

The market in that sense acts like an exchange of goods and services between providers and consumers (Figure 2.1), similar to the way the physical world acts as an exchange of forces and energy between its different entities. Of course, all market activities do take place in some physical location, whether this is a stock market or online (on a server), but for all purposes seeing it as concept space makes it much easier to represent. Prices are traditionally considered the decision mechanisms by which exchanges between sellers and buyers take place. In the traditional economic sense prices refer to monetary values, while in the more expanded view of the market/economy that we will adopt here, prices are only one aspect of the exchange and other forms, such as power, satisfaction and

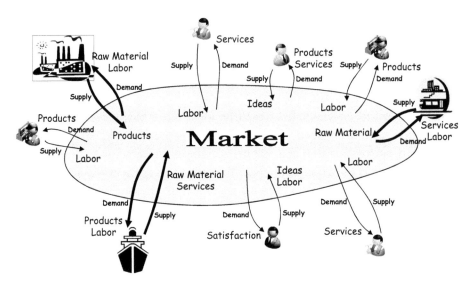

Figure 2.1   The market environment

pleasure, also affect exchanges. If one only wants to deal with monetary prices, the utility of the other types of exchange will have to be converted to price if we are to accurately represent an exchange. Buying for example a jewel could mean a lot more than the price we pay for it, such as, for example, in the case of a wedding ring, which represents commitment and status, among other things.

Utility theory is probably the best approach to include all drivers of supply and demand for products and services. According to that theory, while it is almost impossible to have an objective measure of the utility of a good or service, it is possible to have its comparative evaluation with respect to the alternatives in order of preference to the consumer. Since choices are based on the level of need of a consumer that acts rationally, the tendency to acquire additional units of the same goods or services will remain as long as its marginal utility/ value is equal or greater to the next available alternative.

Utility seen as satisfaction will get us close to what we are trying to achieve in explaining multipreneurship. If we were to consider the creation of business ventures by a multipreneur as adding to an imaginary utility of, say, "business hunger", an entrepreneur will keep expanding an established business as long as it adds to his business hunger and up to the point that the creation of a new type of business becomes more attractive in satisfying his business hunger. Although this approach takes away from traditional economic theory, it does provide us with a way to factor entrepreneurs. Alternatively, we will have to take the existence of markets as given and consider competition as an impersonal process. This would be a simplified approach that ignores the real reason markets are created, which from the beginning of our time is entrepreneurs.

The absence of entrepreneurs as influencers in markets is reflected in traditional economics textbooks as they are heavily focused on a supply and demand analysis (pioneered by Marshal in 1890) and the general equilibrium theory (pioneered by Walras and refined by Arrow and Debreu in 1954). In brief, as the demand for a product or service increases, suppliers will tend to produce more to make more profit. The increased quantities, though, will satisfy the demand, forcing the sellers to reduce the price to attract buyers (Figure 2.2). We have in essence two opposing forces. Something like going to a restaurant. At the beginning you are hungry and willing to pay a lot for the first bites of food, leading the owner to cook more to make you happy and earn money from you. The more you eat, the less hungry you are and the less willing you will be to pay as much as for the first bites, so the owner will begin to reduce the price he is charging you for the remainder. At the same time he needs to reduce the production of food because the market/you doesn't need much anymore. The cycle could repeat again with the same or a different product (such as a sweet, for example).

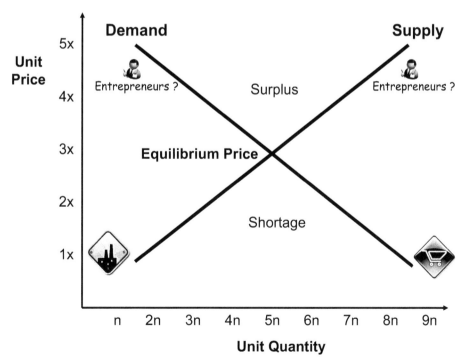

Figure 2.2   The dynamics of supply and demand

Although the traditional approach also recognized the importance of entrepreneurship, the focus on supply and demand leads to confusing positions. Considered as producers, entrepreneurs need to be placed on the supply curve, but if we consider them as distributors and marketers, they are affected by wholesale price and so they need to be on the demand curve. Unless one distinguishes entrepreneurs as producers, distributors and marketers and places them in different curves, this apparent confusing double quality of entrepreneurs led many researchers to avoid considering them in their analysis. In doing so the concept of the market was left to operate with the force of competition between buyers and sellers. In that sense, though, buyers end up competing with other buyers and sellers with other sellers, which in itself is an anomaly to traditional theory, as we usually experience buyers and sellers as passive with respect to other buyers and sellers. Entrepreneurs are usually the ones that produce goods and services at a price that sellers choose to sell and buyers want to buy.

A convenient approach to eliminate confusion would simply be to remove the entrepreneurship from the physical person and assign it to roles. In that sense one can be producer and consumer according to the role they play at

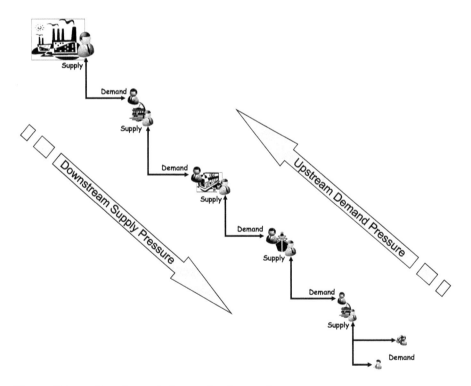

Figure 2.3   Supply and demand roles and pressures

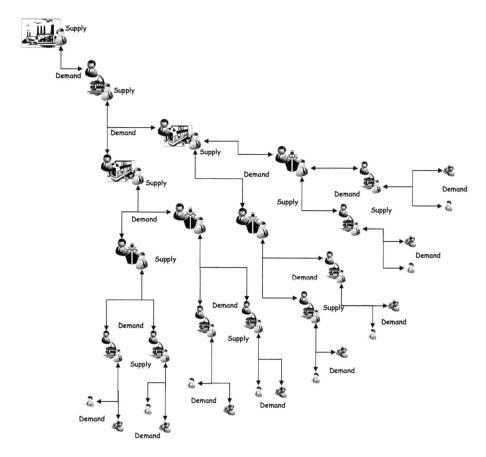

Figure 2.4   Supply and demand roles cascade

each point in time in the market (Figures 2.3 and 2.4). Similarly an entrepreneur can be supplier and consumer at the same time depending on his position in the supply chain. The more upstream one is in the supply chain, the more pure his supplier role is, while the more downstream one is, the stronger the consumer role is. Production is controlled by two opposing forces. Suppliers pressure for higher prices while consumers pressure for lower prices. For each type of product or service, equilibrium is reached when suppliers request what consumers can afford. Product specialization has been devised to target market niches, for example, luxury cars usually target millionaires since they can afford them and want them as a display of status and prestige.

To bring the ideas and concepts presented so far closer to reality, we need to also consider the morphology/structure of a market where all the entrepreneurial activity takes place. The truth of the matter is that regardless of the ease that market abstraction offers in explaining economic activity, we cannot consider it in isolation from other human activities. This is especially true in real life as there is a variety of markets that form the overall economic activity, many of which are closely tied to the natural resources of our physical world. A better way to approach the market idea is to consider a *market space* or market environment where any form of economic activity can be expressed (Figure 2.5).

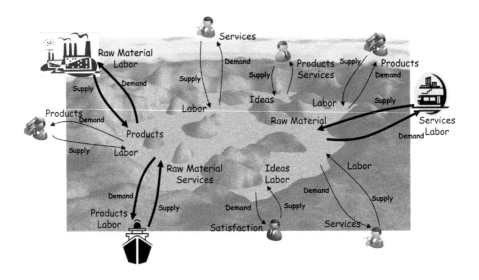

Figure 2.5   Opportunity landscape in markets

The analogy of such a concept with a physical space of mountains and lakes is convenient here. In such physical space water is the equivalent to profit and everything is converted and exchanged as such. Business entities, entrepreneurs, workers and consumers engage in the market space in pursuit of gains/water. Supply provides access to water while demand ensures pumping it out. When the water becomes scarce in one location because the demand exhausted its deposits, supply needs to be directed in drilling it from new areas. This representation—while not crucial for explaining general economic activity and even entrepreneurship—is imperative for an explanation of multipreneurship since by the definition we adopted it's an activity that crosses market/industry boundaries.

Entrepreneurs are the actual shape-changers of the market space by creating more attractive alternatives. By way of the market/lake analogy, it's like drilling wells for water to fill. In doing so other wells might dry up. For example, the money that I spend buying an iPad was really taken from buying a new camera. Apple became richer than Canon. In that sense the amount of water in the market is constant (equal in real life to the available natural resources and the limits of our ingenuity) so one can only change the shape of the lake by making it deeper where his supply goes. In this way water is drained from others areas, making them dry and forming new puddles in others. Often the entrepreneur's effort will be unsuccessful, while at other times it will reward them with more "water". Of course as soon as a well appears, others will converse to exploit it so the real advantage of an entrepreneur is that he has first dips and the option to guard his well from others. Despite his efforts, though, he won't be able to prevent others from drilling nearby and he will end up sharing some of the newly discovered wealth.

2.2   Historic Account

The suggested etymology of the word entrepreneur goes back to its first appearance as the agent noun of *entreprendre*, meaning the undertaker of some activity that later on becomes a business activity. This use evolved to modern times indicating a business creator with the inherent element of risk-taking in exploiting opportunities. In economic theory the term of entrepreneur as a risk-taking specialist was introduced first by the Irish economist of French descent Richard Cantillon in 1755. It was viewed at the time as the person who would compensate workers for labor on a given task according to what consumers were willing to pay. The entrepreneur would assume all the risk as he would have to guess what the consumers would pay at the future time when the task is complete.

This idea was later refined in the US in 1921 by the economist Frank Knight, who distinguished between acceptable and probable risk, which could be accounted for, and uncertainty, which is an unpredictable environmental property. The first case includes events of a known or predictable nature, while the latter required subjective (guessing) estimation of their probability of occurrence. In simple terms, expecting rain in autumn is much more realistic than expecting a hurricane, so one would classify the first as risk and can account for that by taking an umbrella when going out, while the latter is an uncertainty that most people presume won't happen while they are outside. In business it would be like securing your house for fire and not securing it for an asteroid hit. In manufacturing, for example, producing something such as an iPad is working with uncertainty as you can't be sure the market will welcome it. Apple assumed the risk of designing and producing it, gambling on the uncertainty of the market. The decision was successful and allowed the company alone to reap the rewards of the market, reaching unprecedented heights of profit.

By 1934 entrepreneurs became well established and visible in the eyes of their communities, leading Joseph A. Schumpeter to present them as the heroic visionaries who open up new roads in the market, establish new industries and shape the economy in the process. It wasn't the view of the inventor, as much as the view of someone who was creative enough and efficient in moving and manipulating the market to adopt inventions in new and efficient ways. The entrepreneur was the person that would come up with an idea and then find the resources to materialize it. The list of resources could include capital (either personal or from financial institutions) and labor (personal and others), connection and partners.

While the heroic type of entrepreneur is the most memorable and has the greater appeal, theorists need to incorporate the low-level entrepreneurs that are responsible for the great majority of small firms. Their role cannot be ignored as they form the backbone of many economies and greatly contribute to the economic development and growth of many countries. To put their importance into perspective one only needs to consider that most family businesses belong in that category. Andrew Marshall was probably the first to consider this level of entrepreneurship in 1919, but because at the time the available modeling techniques were limited to equilibrium situations (see previous section) their contributions were omitted from the theory of supply and demand.

It wasn't until 1937 when the introduction of the idea of middlemen by Friedrich von Hayek provided an explanation of all types of entrepreneur. In that view entrepreneurs are nothing more than price manipulators engaging in trade. This makes their appearance in market economies evident and explains their lack in socialist economies that are mainly controlled with low-incentive bureaucrats. Profit opportunities are the main motivators for entrepreneurs who seek advantages for price differentiations as buyers (buying low) and sellers (sell high). The difficulty with this approach nevertheless is that it limits the expression of entrepreneurship to simple monetary exchanges. It ignores their vital contribution to the operations of their firm and their involvement in routine decision-making as well as strategic decision making. The latter is an important characteristic of firms and allows manufacturers and innovators to be included as entrepreneurs along with dealers and speculators.

Involvement in decision-making at all levels of a firm creation and operation is a vital aspect of entrepreneurship that any theory needs to address.

An important aspect of entrepreneurship that became apparent later on was its contribution to the continuous, dynamic and sustainable growth of a firm as a necessary ingredient for their maturity and success. Edith T. Penrose in 1955 was the one who pioneered the importance of entrepreneurship in her *Theory of the Growth of the Firm*. Penrose differentiated herself from Marshall's approach in that she considered many of his factors responsible for the rate of growth of the firm and not its size. The internal consistency of her theory was based on the inherent natural predisposition of firms to grow and that entrepreneurship was stronger than resource as a driving factor in that direction. In other words, even if there is an initial lack of resources, entrepreneurs have the ability to counter that by utilizing and expanding their network to reach out and fill any gaps they initially experience.

In addition to growth maximization, Penrose suggested that shareholder value maximization is also an objective of the firm. The latter is seen more in the form of profit maximization in contrast to the former, which is more related to a dividend payout constraint. While these differences might not look significant, they do affect the perspective of a firm from a theoretical point of view as they can imply different strategic approaches. One can look at examples of modern enterprises such as Amazon, which focuses on growth and literally ignores dividends, and IBM, which steadily provides dividend to shareholders. Both companies are overall doing great for stretches of time that spread over decades and beyond economic crisis, leading one to believe that theories should be flexible enough to accommodate the various business realities. This is also the challenge and a threat to rigor for any theory as diversity in the observations resists formalization, at least with the tools we have available nowadays.

As we move closer to our modern-day theories and more specifically to the case of repeat entrepreneurs, which we are interested in here, we see that a lot of emphasis is placed in the human capital and the cognitive mindset of entrepreneurs. In the 1990s human capital theorists came to realize that entrepreneurial behavior is related to the history of an entrepreneur and, more specifically, to the resources and skills they acquire in particular contexts over time that influence future entrepreneurial behavior. According to this approach and considering achieved skills and attributes through learning and experience, the larger the human capital pool the higher the effectiveness and productivity an entrepreneur would display.

2.3 Typology of Entrepreneurs

Classification of entrepreneurs is important for the development of any theory that will describe entrepreneurship. The problem in doing so, in our case, is the diversity of entrepreneurial activity that creates a heterogeneous environment, which is difficult to organize under a common theoretical framework. A major source of the diversity observed stems from the type and degree of past experience of an entrepreneur, especially in the field of business and particularly in business ownership and management. This type of experience has a direct impact on multipreneurs because it allows them access to funding from financial institutions that routinely screen an applicant based on their accumulated experience. This privilege is an additional status of accomplishment that supports the good reputation an entrepreneur gained from successful past ventures.

A motivational element that in many cases has been used in defining various types of entrepreneur in the past has been the "career anchor". This is defined as the self-perceived talents, motives and values that support a person's career. In those, one can include traditional anchors such as the autonomy/independence anchor and the more rare entrepreneurship anchor. The former expresses the desire to be free from the control of others while the latter inspires one in the act of creating something new. That thirst for the new motivates individuals to take risks, to endure hardships and seek personal prominence. While autonomy-orientation is a key drive and motivator for engaging in venture formation in a serial way, the entrepreneurial anchor is believed to be dominant in the case of multipreneurs. In general experienced entrepreneurs are expected to make better decisions, so one would expect that as long as they don't stretch beyond the physical and cognitive limits, success will be more probable in their case.

Experience is a distinct quality that separates entrepreneurs into novices and matures and will be the primary constituent of the typology we will use here. The former category includes those with no prior experience in business ownership, while the latter refers to entrepreneurs who have business ownership experience that they can leverage in their future ventures. Novices usually display experience relating to their current venture, which they presumably acquired by exposure to the details of the particular domain through observation and exposure to aspects of it, as either employees or spectators amongst others (students, trainees, research, etc.). This might be proven a limitation in moving down the experience curve that allows them to identify and exploit opportunities for new ventures. While experience in most cases of multipreneurship is considered an asset, it can in some instances act as a liability, especially if it acts as a block to learning from exposure to new situations. In that sense one should assume that multipreneurs have a tendency to be successful and outperform novice entrepreneurs.

Although the division of entrepreneurs into novice and mature provides a dichotomy that would satisfy most theorists, we want to include here a special category for potential or incubating entrepreneurs (Figure 2.6). This addition will help later on to explain the "ingredients" of entrepreneurial potential and address the need for policy formulation that will increase their supply in the economy. In this category, which forms the precursor of novices, we will include those involved in thinking or planning their venture into entrepreneurship and are in the initial phase of intelligence and information collection. As we will later see, there are important personality traits and environmental characteristics that allow and promote such attitudes, so one should consider them in any framework that attempts to make sense and explain the phenomenon of entrepreneurship. A typical example is in family business where an entrepreneur is incubating (trained and brainwashed) from early on in his life to take over and grow the family business.

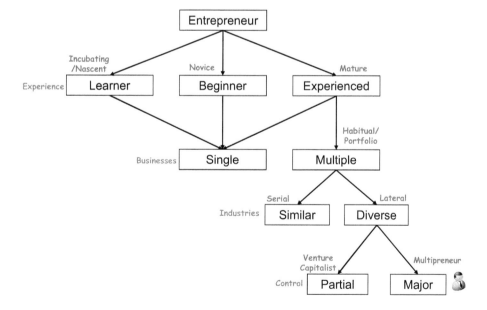

Figure 2.6   Typology of entrepreneurial behavior

While novices by their nature need to focus on the operations and expansion of their single business, mature entrepreneurs often express an interest in creating more ventures. Entrepreneurs of this type are called *habitual* or *portfolio* entrepreneurs and have the tendency to expand into distinctly separate ventures, either concurrently with existing ones or after ending one (closing or selling in whole or in part) and opening another. Dependent on whether the new venture is in the same field as the previous one or in a different one, the entrepreneur is considered *serial* or *lateral*. Of particular interest to this book is the category of lateral entrepreneurs, which is close to the definition of multipreneurship we adopted in the first chapter. A more strict separation based on the ownership percentage of the entrepreneur can split this category into *venture capitalists*, where they have minority and/or majority stakes in more than one business, and the category of *multipreneurs*, who have majority ownership in multiple businesses.

A final distinction that one can find in literature is regarding the magnitude of the entrepreneurial venture. Based on the size of the enterprise one can consider a further division of each of the presented types into low- and high-level entrepreneurs. In the former category one expects to find the traditional entrepreneurs that inherited or started a small business such as a convenience store, a grocery or a bakery, to name a few. These businesses usually target the local population of a neighborhood or a suburb and can even grow to cover their local communities in their cities and even countries. The latter category involves what we also know as high-profile entrepreneurs and includes those who build corporations that stretch beyond national boundaries and have a global reach. Because this division is of primary importance for the case of multipreneurship we study here, we will deal with each one of them separately in the follow-up chapters. For now, it suffices to say that this distinction does not affect the structure of the typology we presented in Figure 2.6, as it addresses an aspect of entrepreneurship that hasn't been dealt with historically, at least with respect to some of the concepts we will discuss later on in this chapter (such as human capital and opportunity exploitation).

The breakdown of entrepreneurs into the types we presented here is neither exclusive nor restrictive and it's of a dynamic nature as it accommodates change over time. It also has a dynamic nature since one entrepreneur can jump to another type and should be seen as a division that can be operationalized. Additional subdivisions can be established based on the success and/or failure rates of the entrepreneurial ventures as well as the types of deal/venture they pursue and the types of team they build. Studying these varieties is beyond the scope of this book, although we believe that the framework we develop in Chapter 6 can easily include many of the variations mentioned.

2.4 The Notion of Rationality

Rationality refers to our ability as self-interested individuals to make choices based on our preferences. While it is of a social nature, it treats exchanges between parties similar to economic exchanges, where everyone is trying to maximize their advantage or gain, which can be either physical (health, profit, etc.) or emotional (satisfaction, among others). By default entrepreneurs, like all human beings, are treated as rational and outcomes are influenced by our cognitive and situational differences.

Some of the types of rationality one encounters in the literature and are of interest in our study of multipreneurs include:

- *Instrumental:* Actions are the result of the adoption of suitable means to an end. In the case of entrepreneurship the actor uses practical reasoning and makes a calculated decision on how to build a new venture. One considers the factors involved in a situation as variables that can be manipulated and allows other things to happen (such as resolve conflicts, gather resources, solve problems and efficiently perform technical tasks). This is the dominant mode of thinking in the industrial world and supports the notion that everything is a matter of resources and that unlimited availability of resources can create almost anything.

- *Situational:* The situation one is experiencing through interactions with people and nature in a particular place and time dictates future action that is retrospectively rational. In simple terms, based on rational choices, a sequence of events will lead someone to actions beneficial to him.

- *Bounded:* The premise here is that there are physical limits (bounds) to cognition that affect rational decision-making and that decision-making is limited by the information individuals have about alternatives and their consequences, the cognitive limitations of their mind and the time available to them to decide. It was developed as an alternative to the algorithmic/mathematical modelling of decision-making that economics and related disciples were promoting. What this says, in simple terms, is that under time pressure individuals will tend to maximize satisfaction instead of searching for the optimum response (by a systematic search of the available options). As a result, the *rule of thumb* will most likely influence decision outcomes rather than an exhaustive analysis of every contingency.

- *Perfect:* This is the ideal form of rationality where the individual is fully informed, perfectly logical and makes the perfect decision that will lead in the case business to maximum economic gain (profit).

While theorists have argued in favor of one form of rationality over another, in the case of entrepreneurs what has proven as a requirement for the identification of opportunities and their exploitation is the exhibition of metacognition. Given that part of cognitive processing is the need to include awareness of thinking about resources and skills, it is necessary for individuals to be aware of their cognitive processes, if they are to consciously switch perspectives between mindfulness and mindlessness in accordance with their thinking stage of the time. Cognitive processing in this respect will be influenced by the innate abilities of each individual and their experience in the area of exposure.

2.5   The Notion of Human Capital

Rationality impacts the quality of judgment people make but it's not as influential to decision-making as the personal characteristics people are born with and those they acquire throughout their lives. These characteristics influence our intellectual capabilities and shape our attitudes and motivations towards economic activities and life in general. Our potential to process information eventually leads some people to make better decisions with less effort than others. If one combines this with personality attributes and the environment in which we operate, we can see why people act the way they act and how some decisions lead to self-employment and the creation of new ventures while others guide them to traditional forms of employment in private or government sectors.

Human capital is usually defined as the potential human beings accrue through their life in terms of qualities and competencies that can support their future economic aspirations and endeavors. In simple terms it is an abstract representation of human beings as transactional agents in economic environments. Although the term has been adopted for economic purposes, one can easily see extensions to its use that would include emotional and spiritual dimensions, especially when these dimensions are known to act as drivers and motivators for the attitudes of an individual towards life and his purpose of being.

Traditional human capital approaches are based, as we mentioned, on the discipline of economics. As such, education and past experience are some of the main contributors to human capital. Education has notably been an important source of knowledge that boosts self-confidence and improves critical thinking and problem-solving abilities. It sharpens the analytic abilities of individuals and advances their skills in anticipating obstacles and devising appropriate strategies to overcome them. Adding experience (especially in venture formation) to the mix of human capital, we can see that in the case of habitual entrepreneurs human capital provides the coping mechanism for entrepreneurs to deal with adversity and succeed in the formation of a new business.

Human capital can be accrued through experience and, in the case of the multipreneurs that we study here, this might be a defining reality for their ability to establish and control diverse ventures. The development of entrepreneurial skills, from the point of view of an individual, includes the ability to identify and exploit opportunities. A lot of times the process of identifying an opportunity is perceived as the process of creating an opportunity. From our perspective, though (which we will see later on), opportunities of every form exist in a space of opportunities and the entrepreneur is there to identify and materialize the promising ones.

Along with entrepreneurial skills, entrepreneurs also need managerial skills, such as the ability to organize people and resources, and technical skills when the venture has technical focus. These skills can be improved from repeated business ownership, especially if a new venture is in the same sector as previous ones. An entrepreneur that already knows a market and the ways to acquire resources will know what to expect and how to get to where he wants to be. In addition, having a reputation in a field will always act in their favor and allow them easier access to critical resources and networks. In that sense, it is much easier for habitual entrepreneurs to accumulate additional human (as well as other) capital and utilize it to build new business.

The accumulation of human capital can be seen as a conscious and calculated process, although it is now believed that cognition should be included. In that respect bounded rationality is probably the better-suited candidate. This allows us to account for the cognitive limits of individuals in information processing and in this respect it makes the inclusion of cognition in human capital a necessity. One can see this as an endowed human capital inherited by their parents and strengthened by the society they live in. In this way cognition and its expression through logic can also be viewed as forms of human capital.

Logic is a form of information funnel through which entrepreneurs filter their attention and prune the conformation space of possibilities.

Although cognition follows the psychological paradigm, it can help explain how information (as brought to attention through sensory stimulation) is processed and stored for later retrieval and use. It also serves as the dominant influence of our performance in decision-making and shapes experience and attitudes towards learning and information processing with an end result in the way we think and act. Differences in cognitive processing help us make sense of the world around us and are at the root of the behavior we display.

Since cognition directly influences decision-making, it is no wonder that it can be shaped by experience. Adjusting judgment is necessary for entrepreneurs and habitual ones make it a "habit" to base decisions on past experience, creating a dynamic circle of learning. Experienced entrepreneurs are bound to have repositories of information that allow them to use heuristics to simplify strategies and make effective decisions in the absence of complete information. In this way, they can outperform novices who lack internal benchmarking capabilities and have to rely on exhaustive and analytical searches to find an optimum strategy to deal with challenges. This effort, by its own nature, costs more, requires time and disadvantages novices with respect to habitual entrepreneurs in competitive situations. This disadvantage could become an advantage for novices in new situations where habitual entrepreneurs might show an over-reliance on heuristics that no longer work in the new domain. The tendency to confirm prior beliefs and overconfidence can constrain one from making correct judgments and act as a barrier to new and potential useful perspectives.

More information on human capital can be found in published research, but the reader who plans to expand on the subject needs to be aware of the assumption usually made in the corresponding academic research. Collecting data on human capital can only be done by direct access to individuals and, since this is not always possible to do, much of the published research is based on proxies such as demographic data. Interpreting human capital profiles in this way is based on stereotypical averages so it doesn't reflect individual characteristics that might be vital in the expression of entrepreneurial behavior.

2.6   The Concept of Opportunity

Opportunity is a strategic concept in entrepreneurship as it relates to the creation of a firm by the entrepreneur. Economists view opportunity as a generic unexploited activity, while in its more simplified form it represents an idea about how to earn profit. It is a very difficult concept to apply in practice, as can be seen from the limited number of successful entrepreneurs in the market compared with the available human potential. Regardless of its definition, many theorists seem to conceive it as a potential unexploited project in contrast to an activity that could be purposeless and casual. Projects inherently have a purpose and their goal is to organize and manage resources to achieve a specific objective that is well defined in time and place. Entrepreneurs can adapt their past project experiences to fit the parameters that define the new ones, forming in this way a hybrid virtual representation of the future project based on the opportunity they identified.

The central role of opportunity in entrepreneurship has been debated a lot, primarily on the argument that if there are dormant opportunities all over the place, why haven't we discovered and exploited them, given that in one way or another resources that could assist in their exploitations can always be found. To counter this perceived inefficiency, the concept of diminishing returns can be of assistance. If all types of opportunities get the same chance at discovery, the ones that cost less are bound to draw more attention and be exploited first. This is the simple law of maximizing profit while minimizing effort. By focusing on the most visible and obvious (easy to discover) opportunities, we increase the cost of discovery of less obvious ones (difficult to discover) as most entrepreneurs will be attracted to the easy ones and fewer resources become available for searching and exploiting the remaining opportunity space.

Duplication of effort almost always follows initial successes as more people want a share of the newly discovered "pie" (well of water in Figure 2.5), leading to a breakdown of the potential profits amongst many. The depletion of the group of similar opportunities during a period of time has another dramatic effect and that is to discourage, in the long run, entrepreneurs from continuing the search and new ones entering the field. Eventually the expected profit cannot outweigh the cost for searching for new opportunities and equilibrium is reached, preventing in this way the exhaustion of that part of the opportunity space during that period of time.

Obviously if the economic environment was static all around the world, there would be a time when we will have exploited all feasible opportunity. This stagnation point, though, is unlikely to exist (anytime soon anyway) as volatility dominates the markets and the world economy always offers new ground for opportunities to exist. In addition, our experience usually grows over time, assisting our intuition and making us more efficient in searching and discovering opportunities. It is almost certain that as the economy adapts to changes, the opportunity space transforms accordingly, changing its landscape in ways that allow new opportunities to surface and become exploitable.

Missing an opportunity or exploiting an unprofitable one is a major challenge for entrepreneurs and it relates to the risk they are willing to take of making a decision on the information they have and the cost of collecting additional information that could lead to a better decision. Additional costs that need to be considered include the acquisition of the "know-how" that helps in the interpretation of information. Education, training and experience can all help one get the ins and outs of a type of trade. This knowledge can support tremendously in evaluating information and identifying the value of opportunities, but it always comes at a cost that impacts the process of making decisions about opportunities. A network of experts can also serve as outsourcers of information processing for the entrepreneur and a substitute for knowledge and skills he is lacking.

Without a theory of evaluating information, entrepreneurs are left to use heuristics, which based primarily on past experience produce fast results but might prove dangerous in new situations. While they offer fast screening of the information space and the signals one receives, they require a solid and proven methodology that is backed by success in multiple settings. The intuitive nature of heuristics is usually formed by impressions we formed (not necessary lived experiences) as we move in life and the role models we observed. In this sense they are always influenced by things that happened and not the ones that will be. It takes a lot of experience for entrepreneurs to be able to spot the ingredients of success out of the background "noise" of economic and personal interactions.

2.7   The Notion of Business Networks

Networks play a crucial role in social sciences and subsequently to theories of entrepreneurship. They form the sources entrepreneurs use to discover and synthesize information that will help them in identifying and exploiting opportunities for profit. Different types of network provide different support to entrepreneurs. Financial institutions and partners, for example, can provide the monetary backing needed to resource a new venture. Physical networks such as transportation and communication networks can provide worldwide trade capabilities, while family and friends can provide emotional support and encouragement to go on.

The theory of networks originates from the theory of graphs in mathematics and is formed upon the notion of connectivity. For the purposes of this book we will make limited use of their formal representations and focus on their basic characteristic, which is to connect *elements/nodes* based on *relationships/edges*. These two basic ingredients of networks allow for complex structures of elements and relationships to emerge, making them ideal in expressing social structures. In the case of entrepreneurship and economics in general we will move away from the pure mathematical interest on network configuration and introduce a variety of elements that express the different entities involved in the discovery of opportunity and the formation of ventures to exploit them (Figure 2.7).

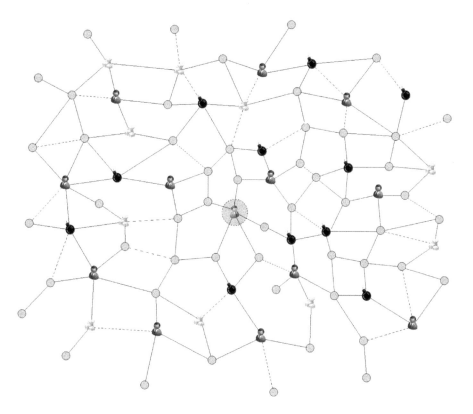

Figure 2.7   The entrepreneur as a hub in the network space

From the entrepreneurship point of view some of the characteristics of networks that contribute to their importance as a theoretical tool include their size, diversity of elements, the types of relationships and the patterns the different interconnected elements form. Additional characteristics that play an important role in the description of entrepreneurship include the concepts of hubs, webs and that of redundancy. The latter refers to the number of alternative paths that exist between two elements in the network. While redundancy may sound wasteful, in reality it impacts flexibility as it provides alternative ways in entrepreneurship to accomplish the exploitation of an opportunity. It also allows the formation of new linkages to be expressed that can modify a path to make it profitable.

Hubs are elements that make more than two connections with other elements (such as the entrepreneur in Figure 2.7) and in an economic perspective they act as consolidation and distribution centers for the traffic over the network. Their importance and power of influence (centeredness in math terms) can be measured by the amount of traffic that originates or terminates in them. This is relevant not only to the number of relationships they make (size) but also on the strength (or bandwidth in a traffic) of those relationships.

While hubs are good in expressing inflow and outflow, they lack redundancy that, as we mentioned before, provides the flexibility entrepreneurs need for building their firms. An elimination of a link completely cuts off access between the elements it was connecting and can lead to fatal failure for the hub unless other hubs have already been established that can take over the diverted traffic (similar to how the Internet works). The latter case shows the formation of a web where there are many ways to connect two elements. An additional disadvantage of the hubs is that they are prone to congestion that slows down flow, especially when traffic becomes unidirectional. More like city traffic where congestions are observed in the morning when everyone gets in the city and in the afternoon when everyone leaves their work to go home. The analogy shows the central role entrepreneurs can play in networks and the skill they might need to control the information traffic that flows through them. Congestion in their case can either cause physical overhead in handling the traffic and/or informational overhead to coordinate proper routing of every signal.

Despite the limitations of hubs for intermediation and the coordination of trade, they are preferable in many ways and especially when it comes to policy formations, as they are more feasible economically than webs. Introducing a new element in a hub means it needs to form connections only with the elements it is meant to connect with, while a new element in a web needs to connect with all the other elements in the web, making it economically much more expensive.

Confusion sometimes stems from the way networks are used to express a variety of situations because of the types of elements one uses to express different aspects of economic activity. A network can be seen as an organizational form that acts as intermediary between the firm and the market or as a network of subsidiaries or as a network of networks or, in an entrepreneurial sense, as a business network of the key actors involved in the discovery and exploitation of opportunities (bankers, government officials, supplier, customers, etc.). For the purposes of this book we will consider all these varieties as different types of network and not as alternative representations. In addition, the notion of networks as tools that explain a phenomenon will be adopted instead of considering them as phenomenon for explanation.

Networks offer an elementary advantage in describing social entities as they allow aggregation of elements at different levels. Single units can be organized in groups and abstracted, allowing the representation of firms as separate entities (see Figures 2.9 and 2.10). Similarly, geographic groupings such as a city or a region can be incorporated, allowing representation of flows of material and information and facilitating analysis of industrial complexes. At the social level networks provide an advantage in representing the spread of qualities such as reputation and trust along with flow connections such as a call for participation or the communication of a message (as in marketing).

Entrepreneurs in networks are usually represented as information hubs that service consumers and compete with other entrepreneurs for custom. In such a role they might contact a producer to produce a good or service that customers requested. In the role of a leader they might instead facilitate intermediation to bring parties together, acting in this way as a bridge. In a similar way, otherwise disparate elements can form their own connections and compete with the entrepreneur for influence over the members' views.

2.8   The Notion of Social Capital

Representing social value is arguably a real challenge for any theoretical framework and the case of multipreneurs is no exception to the rule. The issue is mainly one of representing social interaction between rational multiple actors in different settings. In that respect social capital is nothing more than the value one can derive from participating and interacting with social networks. These networks can be seen as a special category of networks where each element is a person connected to other persons through relationships that can range from family to friends, to social groups such as clubs and associations, to colleagues and people in organizations and business (Figure 2.8).

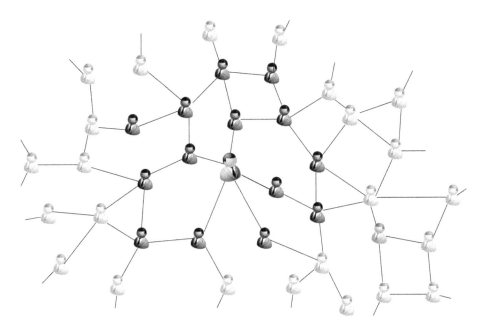

Figure 2.8   The entrepreneur as a hub in the social network space

One can say that entrepreneurial networks are nothing more than social networks in that even when dealing with organizations or governments, one is still dealing with people who happen to be expressing organization intent, either as leaders or as representatives of the organization. Having a good reputation and relating to a bank manager can assist one in getting a loan from that bank, so from an analysis point of view the bank can be represented by a person and the relationship with the entrepreneur can represent any constraints the policies might impose. The evident advantage for the entrepreneur here for being part of the network with the bank manager and in general in other networks is the added value the social class adds to enabling transactions. In such a way social capital as represented through the social network can be a great source of credibility and support and can add great market value over time to the entrepreneur.

One important characteristic of social networks, exactly like the more mathematical networks we have seen before, is their dynamic nature. Elements can appear, forming new relationships with existing elements in time, and disappear, eliminating the paths to contacts. Because they appear to change their shape under no control from anywhere, networks are said to behave as "self-organizing". In reality it is the evolution of the environment and its interactions with the elements of the network that shapes and reorganizes the network. We are not considering here transitory networks, where people may just come together on occasion (say a celebration or a football match). The relationships there are temporary and will diminish after the event. We are interested here in long-term relationships that persist over time in the form of a network. A special requirement for this to happen is the replenishment of lost members with new ones. An appropriate physical representation would be the pool of water (a lake probably) we mentioned in the discussion of economics, where as the water dries, rain can bring up more, renewing in this way the pool and keeping it full.

Social capital can affect economic performance in a variety of levels or social circles (Figure 2.9). The innermost circle is normally formed by the extended family of the entrepreneur and can serve in many cases as an intergenerational finance system. It eliminates in this way the need for financing from external sources that can complicate and even prohibit entrepreneurial venture activities. In other cases the individuals in this circle can act as a support system for taking away family responsibilities and allowing the entrepreneur to focus his time on the pursuit and exploitation of opportunities.

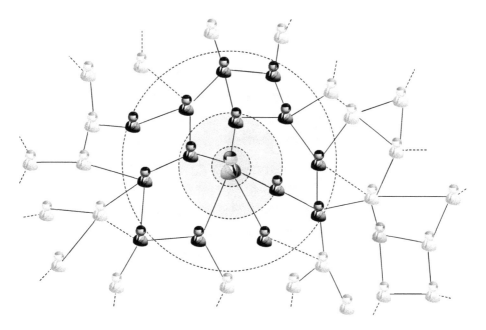

Figure 2.9   Social circles of influence

An outer social circle might represent the local business community of the entrepreneur, where the various stakeholders know and interact with each other (Figure 2.9). This circle can provide partners and supporters for the

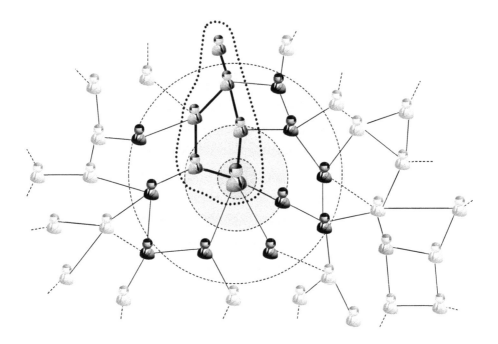

Figure 2.10   Group formation in social networks

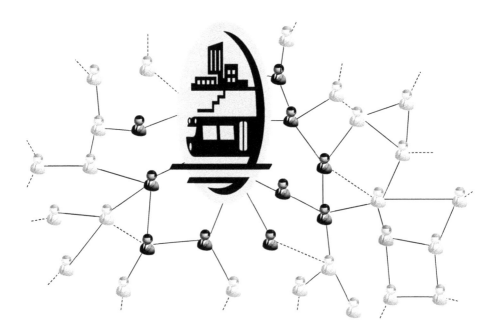

Figure 2.11   Enterprise in social networks

entrepreneur. The larger the circle, the more nodes it will include and the greater the advantage of its structure will be, allowing the entrepreneur to emerge as an influential leader. Using his position the entrepreneur can exert influence over other members to achieve his goals. Certain parts of the networks will be reinforced in this way and persist over time (Figure 2.10). They will eventually be identified as a group glued together by their distinct characteristics and interests and under the title of an enterprise or a social entity. This enterprise for all purposes can now be dealt with as an independent element within the original network (Figure 2.11).

The glue that keeps individuals in business organizational structures is trust. It acts as an enhancer of relationships that effectively reduces 'social distance' to allow individuals to gain power in numbers and expertise. The deeper meaning of trust is that of predictability in favor of support and commitment to honor obligations. The strength of trust and the ease of communication that a network structure allows are the primary determinants of the formation of aggregate elements such as businesses. Anything that supports the spread of trust, such as reputation, common cultural background and joint experiences, can act as an effective support mechanism for entrepreneurs.

The contribution of social capital to entrepreneurship should be evident by now. Considering it in relation to the notions of opportunity identification and exploitation, we can see its influence in creating new ventures that exploit or even create market opportunities. Social capital is a great resource in collecting information about potential opportunities and it can provide contacts that will commit their resources for exploiting the opportunity. The influence of trust is vital at these stages, as in addition to bringing the selected members of the social network of the entrepreneur together, it ensures confidentiality to maximize a share of the market and the return on the investment. The savings from utilizing social capital are multiple in this way and, apart from the monetary contributions, they include economies of effort and time. Without them, the entrepreneur would need to devote energy in building the network required to support his activities.

In addition to assisting in opportunity exploitation and resource acquisition, social capital is also a valuable tool in market organization, especially in large-scale entrepreneurial activity. This is especially true when innovative products or services are involved that need physical outlets for distribution into the market. Innovation is desirable in general because it reconfigures the market, expanding it in a way, allowing more diversity and new entrants that overall can increase economic activity. The entrepreneur needs to compete with existing products or services and divert market attention to his, affecting in this way the morphology of the market. To succeed in turning customers away from the competition, the entrepreneur's business needs to build trust with consumers. This will be done by advertising, by displaying the product or service at convenient locations and discounted initial offerings. In this way trust will be communicated and loyalty will be built. The social capital of the entrepreneurial venture will rise, leading to further increase in market share for the entrepreneur.

2.9   Habitual Entrepreneurs

Based on research findings, the theoretical elements we presented here can be brought together to explain some of the differences observed between the various types of entrepreneurs and, more specifically, the multipreneurs we study here. The strongest probable factor in predisposing someone towards entrepreneurship is tradition. This is evident by the many cases of individuals whose parents are already business owners. Walking into a familiar territory provides strong incentives, as one might already be exposed to the skills and competencies required for such activities. In addition, individuals can easily take advantage of the existing business reputation and the network of contacts the family business has developed over the years. The managerial skills that are required for successful involvement in businesses need time to be acquired, so one that is already immersed in the business world has an early advantage over others who will need years to acquire them.

The lack of family business exposure is compensated by many portfolio entrepreneurs by being in managerial positions before venturing as entrepreneurs and in many cases from being in more than one organization. The time spent in leadership teams and the exposure one gets in different organizational structures allows one to be familiar with firm operations and the build-up of successful teams. This knowledge is also reflected in the fact that many of the portfolio entrepreneurs are quite comfortable and actually seek to include equity partners in their firms. Knowing their cognitive and skill limitations and establishing management teams that can complement each other seems to be one of the greatest assets of habitual entrepreneurs. In addition they learn early on to effectively delegate responsibility to partners with greater depth of experience and access to wider networks.

Prior business ownership is a strong element in expanding to new business ventures, not only because of the financial and network support it provides but also because it puts in proper perspective the evolution and expectations entrepreneurs have from the new ventures. Experience can make someone more cautious as they already know the daunting efforts required to build an enterprise and the risks involved. Network formation is also not such a priority to serial entrepreneurs as it is to novices as they are more focused on capitalizing and maximizing the use of their existing networks. Experienced entrepreneurs tend to also be more conservative in their expectations of control and the future direction of the market, probably due to the fact they have experienced a lot more market changes in their lifetime than novices.

Regarding what triggers one to become serial entrepreneurs versus a novice, some of the similarities include the desire for independence, autonomy and wealth creation. These motivations might be supplemented with more materialistic ones as someone transitions from novice to serial entrepreneur and, in the case of portfolio entrepreneurs, might include the sense of security diversification provides and a sense of excitement and fulfillment from engaging in diverse activities. The last element is evident in many cases and will be apparent in follow-up chapters as it is associated with the thrill of meeting a challenge and being competitive.

Materializing a business formation for portfolio entrepreneurs is based strongly on finding the right talent and forming the team. This makes sense as the diversity of their ventures requires diverse talents that it's unlikely they will possess. Portfolio entrepreneurs tend to be more delegators and, in this respect, they tend to establish a culture of innovation across all levels of their organizations by introducing and engaging innovative people. The truth behind this attitude is that they have already proven their worth with previous successful ventures, so they don't feel threatened or challenged by the competency and creativity of others. In fact, they cherish innovative individuals and try to exploit their talent by promoting them and expanding their roles. Growing their people is vital for portfolio entrepreneurs as it helps grow their enterprises and ensure their stakes in them. They are also more demanding when it comes to performance issues as they more directly relate employed productivity to profit.

Opportunity search and exploitation is another area that habitual entrepreneurs have mastered well. Prior experience proves to be an asset in searching for the appropriate information and engaging the sources their networks provide. These types of entrepreneur seem to believe that almost anything could be made into an opportunity if one can access the right kind of resources and engage the right kind of people. Even when the exploration of an opportunity seems to result in nothing, experienced entrepreneurs believe it would lead to other opportunities, eventually reaching one that will be turned into a profitable reality. Self-awareness about their ability to organize resources, build teams and coordinate tasks is one of the strong personal characteristics of experience entrepreneurs. Organizing a business is probably a skill habitual entrepreneurs can bring from one business to another. If we could attribute some skill to them, in addition to identifying and exploiting opportunities, it is their organizational capability that, coupled with the proper team selection and empowerment, will eventually lead to success. In that respect they are excellent project managers.

Comparing serial and lateral entrepreneurs we can observe their slight difference in information needs. Serial entrepreneurs seem to be more specialized in a field and this leads them to personally seek more in-depth information about new ventures before committing. Lateral ones on the other hand rely more on the domain expertise and advice others might provide and especially other business owners. This is also in relation to the expertise of the entrepreneur, as serial ones seem to believe their technical expertise in their area is one of their great strengths while portfolio entrepreneurs are generalists by nature. In addition, the specialization of the serial entrepreneur seems to anchor them towards specific search patterns within their industry and at times this works against them in identifying potential opportunities. One might think they are predisposed to certain aspects of the market, restricting their view and overanalyzing business opportunities.

The investment characteristics of habitual entrepreneurs are also a significant difference over the other types of entrepreneurs. Portfolio entrepreneurs in general seem to invest more total initial capital for new business formation, a lot of which they gather from external sources by capitalizing on their reputation. They also seem to leverage the financial resources of their various businesses in the pursuit and exploitation of opportunities. In some cases, though, the opposite is observed and a risk-averse behavior over time emerges in some in an effort to preserve their wealth and status among their peers and their communities.

2.10   Are Entrepreneurs Born or Made?

Research indicates that some individuals are innately predisposed to recognize entrepreneurial opportunities, engage in entrepreneurial activity and perform well at running their own business. Moreover, it has also been shown that personality characteristics mediate genetic effects on the recognition of opportunities, the decision to be an entrepreneur and the performance at entrepreneurial activity. This evidence of biological underpinnings of entrepreneurship complements environmental explanations of why people become entrepreneurs and what accounts for entrepreneurial performance. As a result, it improves our understanding of entrepreneurship and the normative implications we can draw from our research on it. However, much additional work is required in order to better understand how genes influence entrepreneurial behavior, both alone and in interaction with environmental stimuli.

The greatest quality of an entrepreneur that most theories will support is good judgment in decision-making. This is an indicator of a rational person's ability to draw a sound conclusion in the absence of complete information. Judgment is the outcome of synthesizing different types of information from different sources and reaching a conclusion. The availability of sources is vital in providing a variety of information to the entrepreneur, so the network they build is of primary importance in supporting their decision-making process. Network formation, while a predominant acquired trait, grows and flourishes when entrepreneurs express certain personality traits. Being open-minded and a people person are vital qualities for being network-oriented, while in addition helps one see opportunities that would otherwise be missed and getting proper advice and support from others.

Based on the decisions they make, entrepreneurs explore profit opportunities. Competition rewards decision-makers with good judgment and penalizes those without. Volatility in the environment is an environmental condition that allows for change and subsequently the creation of opportunities although, in dramatic cases, at a pace entrepreneurs cannot handle. The impact of change is vital as it changes the market landscape and reveals opportunities that were not available or visible before. Entrepreneurs have the inherent ability to observe and spot these new opportunities and convert them into profitable ventures.

As the case studies we will look at in the next chapters will show, entrepreneurs and especially multipreneurs place a strong emphasis on execution. This element, with appropriate marketing and strict quality control, can make a business grow. Other traits that support entrepreneurial behavior include a predisposition towards creativity and innovation and strong leadership in building and managing the core team that will launch a new venture.

Answering a question of whether entrepreneurs are born or made might prove to be like the question of whether artists are born or made. Can anyone be Picasso, Mozart or Michelangelo? It goes without saying that something has to be there. Would we expect someone who is 3 feet tall to be an NBA basketball player? Would we bet money, training everyone at similar heights, to discover the next Michael Jordan? To make it more intellectual, would we expect everyone to be a good poker player? Even if we were to train everyone to the maximum of their abilities, there will still be some people who can more easily remember cards and pick up the behavioral signals of others. Let's see if the following chapters can provide any evidence to the contrary.

Chapter 3
Low-level Multipreneurship

The majority of business activities, at least concerning the engagement in managerial endeavors, involve the class of entrepreneurs that are usually identified as micro-entrepreneurs or low-level entrepreneurs (used interchangeably from here on). The "low" is not meant here to indicate significance but rather the revenue levels of those involved, which are usually sufficient enough to support the entrepreneur and the small team that might be supporting him. Given the engagement levels of this low-end entrepreneurship and the fact that the poorer a country is the more people engage in entrepreneurship out of necessity, it is no wonder that the great majority of entrepreneurs are micro-entrepreneurs, who tend in addition to operate informally. The need to ensure survival and make ends meet drives many of those entrepreneurs to engage in multiple activities. In this way they are literally acting as micro-multipreneurs.

An example of low-level entrepreneurship is the establishment of a convenience store, to stock a range of products that are frequently needed in households in the neighborhood of the store. The cognitive load for the entrepreneur in such a case is high at the beginning when critical decisions need to be made regarding the location and function of the store, while at a later stage only routine operational decisions will be needed to maintain and run the business. Judgmental decisions will be still required to address changes in the preferences of the customer or the entry of a local rival, but all of this will be expressed in large timeframes, giving the entrepreneur enough time to plan his strategy and react.

In other cases, such as, say, setting up a small restaurant or takeaway by a cook, in addition to being a good cook, the entrepreneur needs to be able to handle finance issues (ensure funding, keeping books), supplier issues, human resources issues (hiring, insuring and training personnel), marketing and promotional issues and even artistic issues such as decorating the store. Adding to that the short operational horizon of micro-entrepreneurs that is in the hours, days and weeks and comparing it with the quarters and years of a multinational, we can see that one lives in the immediate and constantly changing "now", while the other lives in the much slower-changing global business world.

All this might sound trivial compared with the issues a conglomerate is facing, but, nevertheless, all the basic understanding of the various functional elements of a business must be there. This is easier said than done for a single individual and will have to come naturally and by instinct to him, given that the alternative of gaining them through education and training will need many lifetimes. Another possible explanation for the existence of low-level entrepreneurs is maybe that all these traits are not required in their expert levels and possible deficiencies in one or another can be compensated or supplemented by common logic and/or circumstantial factors. The case of multipreneurship that we are studying here is by default ensuring the elimination of the circumstantial factor since the existence of multiple ventures would have smoothed out chance to a great extent.

A case in point is the way low-level entrepreneurs promote their business. Promotional efforts rely a lot on word of mouth, with contributions from marketing efforts by fliers, banners, referrals, sales presentations and newspaper advertising. The problem with these strategies is that because the micro-entrepreneur is already engaged in the operational details of his business and the day-to-day crisis he might be facing, any effort to promote will have to come second to attending to the more vital operational needs of the business. More extensive forms of promotion, such as radio and TV, apart from requiring time also require money—something that is a scarcity in most cases.

Another influential factor that differentiates this category of entrepreneurs from their high-level counterparts is the economic aspects of starting a business. Initially financing is usually done here from personal savings and support from relatives and friends. In many cases governments provide micro financing that would allow small enterprises to grow and potentially reach stable higher positions. Although this financing is important, it doesn't appear to be restrictive for the majority of successful entrepreneurs. Many times the government agencies and banks that support these initiatives are motivated by social rather than economic reasons (such as reducing unemployment). The result in such cases may be a surplus of entrepreneurs by necessity rather than by choice. The motivation factor, as one would expect, can be quite significant.

To prepare themselves for the economic activities they engage in, low-level entrepreneurs build their own training and education plans. They mostly do that by following the news and market developments, joining affiliate programs, seeking advice and by attending training seminars and presentations by public officials and other entrepreneurs. Advancing to multipreneurship is another challenge that education is unlikely to help since it requires a paradigm shift from specialist to generalist that many cannot handle.

The academic challenge in presenting and analyzing low-level multipreneurs traditionally lies in the "size" of the activity. It is small enough to allow one to clearly see the characteristics that separate the small enterprise from those of the entrepreneur who contributed to its creation and evolution over time. In our case, though, the fact that we are studying multipreneurs (whenever we can distinguish them at this low level) takes away the influence of the characteristics of the firm since multipreneurs succeed in multiple industries. We logically expect in our case that the influence of the person will be dominant and will drive the phenomenon more than anything else.

Despite our confidence in eliminating the influence of the industry specifics, we cannot do the same with the environmental conditions that are supportive of multipreneurship. For that purpose we will later on present a variety of national environments, hoping that the specific role the environment plays will surface.

3.1   The Economic Aspects of Micro-entrepreneurs

The drives behind the choice to become self-employed and venturing to entrepreneurship can be different for each individual and can be affected by personality traits and the environment one lives and operates in (Figure 3.1). In general we tend to have two categories of factors that drive entrepreneurship—the positive ("pull" factors) and the negative ("push" factors). One can be attracted/pulled to an activity or forced/pushed to engage out of necessity. Well-known factors that attract someone to entrepreneurship include the need to be independent and in control, to secure an income, the potential to exploit a market opportunity for profit, tradition, the joy of creating something new and even an attempt to seek excitement. Factors that "push" to entrepreneurial behaviors include unemployment, the need to secure a viable income, and lack of flexibility and alternatives among others. Tradition (inheriting a family business) is another factor that, depending on the person and the situation, can make the engagement either attractive or necessary.

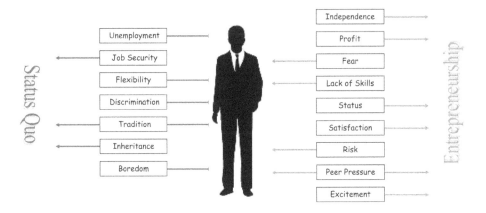

Figure 3.1   Pull and push entrepreneurial drivers

The ongoing decline of the manufacturing sector in many industrial economies and the vast expansion of the services and retail sectors drove most of the losses in traditionally secure middle-class jobs. These jobs were providing sufficient income for consumers to spend in the market, sustaining in this way many businesses and contributing to the economic growth of their societies. Additional factors that contributed to the destruction of the middle class include the changes in technology, politics and trade patterns. Less educated workers have been hit harder than any other group, accepting low-quality jobs. This led to great reductions in incomes to the point that many people rely now on unemployment benefits and minimum wage jobs, with fewer if any benefits and less job security. This situation acted as a push for many individuals to explore and engage in entrepreneurial activity in an effort to supplement and sustain their living standards.

The outsourcing of jobs, which many manufacturers choose to do, to lower-cost nations and the reliance on temporary workers is a related trend to the one we mentioned previously. The pressure to remain competitive, in a world that eliminated distances and cultural barriers, is the drive behind such strategies by corporations. Scaling their workforce up or down with temporary workers allows corporations to respond to demand fluctuations without incurring costs. This combination of outsourcing and relying on a contingent workforce has a positive side-effect to entrepreneurship as it created business opportunities for those willing to take on the outsourcing and provide the services organizations need. The competition of course is fierce and it mainly comes from parts of the world where operational costs are low. Despite this negative implication, the situation nevertheless can be seen as a business opportunity that, with proper planning and sourcing, could provide employment and profit to potential entrepreneurs.

The steep economic environment had another implication, this time on the family structure and dynamics, with the need nowadays for both parents to work and provide income. Balancing family responsibilities and work is becoming a real challenge, especially for working mothers since it impacts on the healthy growth of their children. Under these circumstances self-employment appeared as a way for caregivers to work and at the same time stay close to those in need. The flexibility of working hours (usually around school or day-care schedules) and having a better balance between work and family makes self-employment attractive even if that results in lower income. Similar to that, minorities (such as immigrants and people with disabilities) that would otherwise be excluded from the regular workforce can afford to operate as entrepreneurs on their own.

Immigration and its internal form, urbanism, have shifted population groups that seek better employment opportunities from low-income and no-opportunity areas to higher-income urban centers and wealthier countries with stronger economies. Moving out of their country of origin into a new and more advanced society presents immigrants with opportunities and challenges. The difficulty of being integrated into the native workforce (that is probably already struggling to keep its own population engaged) leads a lot of immigrants to be self-employed and operate small businesses in their local communities. Additional barriers to integration, such as language, culture and education level, create a further push towards entrepreneurship as a way to make ends meet. The decline of many rural economies that created an out-migration had an unexpected "push" effect towards entrepreneurship for those that chose to stay behind (forced to stay probably by strong family and/or cultural ties). In an effort to accumulate sufficient income to sustain themselves, people had to exploit a variety of sources and forms of employment away from traditional farming activities.

The general economic restructuring and the shifting of the population had a positive effect on the creation of new market opportunities, especially in areas not covered by big corporations. Such cases include the gentrification of the urban community, where specialty products and services are requested by high-paying consumers, and the emergence of ethnic enclaves, where demand for culturally specific products and services is high (such as food items, clothes, ritual services etc.). These opportunities create a "pull" effect and are naturally exploited by micro-entrepreneurs.

A controlled factor that also pushes individuals towards entrepreneurship is government and state policies aimed at supporting business creation that will employ citizens in creative and engaging jobs. This is a far better idea than providing unemployment benefits, as it contributes to the economic growth of a suffering population and addresses the psychological and social needs of individuals for self-worth and self-esteem while providing a sense of purpose and belonging. The policies and programs established in such a way can also address minority needs such as those of the disabled and the aging population. Workers over the age of 50 and even younger ones face stiff competition from the young people that enter the workforce since they tend to be viewed as potentially unhealthy, tired and not worth investing in due to the limited productive time they have left. For some reason, this is a notion that even governments passively promote in efforts to reduce the pressure they receive from these groups of the population. Self-employment is often the only option left for aging individuals that need to work to support themselves and their families. Forced retirement also contributes to even older individuals engaging in self-employment.

For a micro-entrepreneur a major concern is the economic feasibility of their start-up until and up to the point where it can sustain itself. Initially financing is usually done from personal savings and support from relatives and friends. In many cases governments provide micro-financing that would allow small enterprises to grow and potentially reach stable higher positions. Although this financing is important, it doesn't appear to be restrictive for the majority of successful entrepreneurs. Many times the government agencies and banks that support these initiatives are motivated by social (such as reducing unemployment) rather than economic reasons. The result in such cases may be a surplus of entrepreneurs by necessity rather than by choice. The motivation factor as one would expect can be quite significant.

As becomes apparent from the factors presented above, the microenterprise sector can be an important component for a local economy and provide solutions that can benefit the social good and ensure the political stability of nations. The economic and demographic forces that shape today's economic landscape can create positive and negative pressure that could drive entrepreneurial attitudes of citizens and provide an outlet for engagement in constructive ways. The changes we observe globally will probably persist in the future and even intensify in many cases, making the engagement of individuals in entrepreneurial endeavors a necessity that is here to stay.

3.2 The Specifics of Low-level Entrepreneurs

From what we have presented so far it should be evident that, if nothing else, micro-entrepreneurs are self-employed individuals who make a business out of multitasking. Critical functions that are normally addressed by many different specialists in regular businesses are addresses by a single individual. While some support might exist, the majority of decision-making is on the entrepreneur. If we could summarize the issues that a micro-entrepreneur needs to address, the list would include:

- functioning as a one-person start-up

- building a portfolio of his brands or, in case he is a commodity, setting up competing prices

- building a customer base

- financing your ventures

- using the Internet

- sustaining a changing lifestyle.

Primary activities of the micro-entrepreneur involve attending to the daily needs and emergencies of the business, such as order fulfillment, supplier communication, customer services, staff recruitment and training, dealing with the legal and financial aspects of the operations and networking, among others. Activities that are found in traditional businesses, such as marketing, often look out of reach of the business owners as they are caught up in the daily and weekly challenges they face.

Promoting a business usually involves low-end means such as word of mouth, fliers and banners, making sales pitches and seeking referrals, although some mass media promotions such as local radio and newspapers might also be involved. The cost of more influential media such as TV advertising is usually prohibited, in addition to being mostly wasted as most low-level enterprises target their close and local communities unless they are expanding. An Internet presence and advertising is usually in the same category.

Training and education in business operations is usually limited for micro-entrepreneurs. Attending seminars, training and becoming members of professional associations and affiliate programs are some of the means used in expanding their knowledge base. Leveraging on them, though, will require moving to the next level, when they begin to employ others and expand their business.

An important aspect that often fails to draw attention is that when competing on the entrepreneurial battlefield many if not most entrepreneurs will fail. And this will be regardless of any training or support they might get from family, friends and/or the state. Any competition will result in some winning and others losing. In that respect entrepreneurs can learn a lot from athletes. Unless they enjoy the ride, engaging in entrepreneurship will most likely be an unpleasant experience, not to mention costly in terms of effort and time. And no one knows this better than multipreneurs. If we were to take this position at a higher level, if a country manages to increase the production of successful entrepreneurs, another will lose. Having the skills and strength to recover from setbacks is vital for successful multipreneurs and the low-level ones are no exception.

A special type of entrepreneurial activity that surfaced in the new millennium is the one that relates to the Internet world. The technology and communications revolution enabled individuals to act as online entrepreneurs (the author included). The Internet, with its social networking capabilities, and the global economic crisis and unreliable job market, forces a lot of individuals (with skills in using the medium) to explore and engage in a radical new way of revenue creation by becoming, in essence, their own conglomerate and brands. While this new form is mainly online, it has spilled over to the physical world when the boundaries converge.

These new single-person conglomerates offer their customers diverse skills and expertise as personal or professional services. The offerings can range from online products and services such as website design, content creation (writing, videos, etc.), consulting, instruction and training to promoting and selling physical products such as handcrafts and art pieces, used and new material and products and music, to mention a few. The online-mediated business model has emerged out of nowhere as individual entrepreneurs driven by unemployment and underemployment discovered its potential to reach across the vast markets of the world.

3.3   Selected Cultural Perspectives

While many of the characteristics of multipreneurs might be universal, the way they interact can be highly idiosyncratic. Even in countries such as China and Russia that transition from strong institutionalization to more competitive market structures, differences can be extreme. An example of such differences is the network sizes and density that vary from culture to culture as well as the levels of trust among the connecting nodes. Chinese networks, for example, tend to persist over time due mainly to the institutional stability of the country and include the close social circle of family, friends and colleagues of the entrepreneur. Russian entrepreneurs, on the other hand, have become mobile to strengthen their networks and build new ones as the transition of the country to a free market left an institutional chaos behind it. Network density is another cultural factor that influences entrepreneurial behavior. If we take again the example of the two countries, we can see that Chinese networks tend to be relatively closed in order to reduce uncertainty compared with the Russian networks, which do not experience close ties amongst members. This makes the Chinese more trustworthy toward third parties when they are accompanied with proper references, while Russian entrepreneurs perceive three-person relationships as risky. These network characteristics offer valuable lessons and strongly affect the ways one must use to break through.

In order to give a flavor of low-level entrepreneurship and multipreneurship across the world and highlight its apparent and potentially stereotypical cultural characteristics, a presentation of its impact in various countries across the globe will follow. The list is meant to include countries from the different classifications the World Economic Forum follows into factor-driven (countries that are mainly agricultural with low economic development), efficiency-driven (industrial countries with visible national economies of scale) and innovations-driven economies (advanced countries with large service sectors that cater to affluent populations). The attempt here is merely to present a representative but obviously not exhaustive reference to attributes and personality traits entrepreneurs and subsequently multipreneurs display. For all purposes one should consider the sample as a convenience sample that aims to bring out the common and distinct characteristics of the self-employed and small businesses that persist across cultures and nations. The cases attempt to emphasize societal characteristics and influences more than anything else, as individual characteristics will be discussed in the following chapter. All the statistical references come from records of the last decade and the primary source in many cases is the Global Entrepreneurship Monitor.

Major characteristics that describe entrepreneurship in cultural/country contexts include, among others:

- educational support for understanding entrepreneurship (knowledge and skills) all the way up through higher education

- skills necessary for the starting and managing ventures along with understanding of market structures and operations: these skills can be acquired through formal education and through experience, training and exposure to entrepreneurial instances

- individualism and cultural esteem of the entrepreneurial vocation as a valued aspect in the society: acting alone and taking responsibility for acting alone is a primary characteristic of entrepreneurs and the value a society places in such a role can support or suppress entrepreneurial behavior

- financial resources available for funding entrepreneurs

- government policies and public programs for entrepreneurship at the national and local levels

- import of know-how and transfer of technology from public research institutions to entrepreneurship

- supporting infrastructure for the availability of affordable and high-quality legal, professional and commercial services

- supporting physical infrastructure, mainly in the transportation and communication areas, at acceptable costs for new entrepreneurs

- market openness, referring to the ease of entry of new entrepreneurs into a market: this is vital in allowing entrepreneurs to exploit business ideas by building and managing their own businesses

- intellectual property rights protection for private ownership of knowledge.

AUSTRALIA

Australia is a country rich in natural resources that managed to cultivate an entrepreneurial culture that engages about 10.5% of its adult population in entrepreneurship, ranking the country second to the US among the developed countries. Half of them are even involved in developing or launching new products, indicating that the quality of entrepreneurial activities is high. This is also reflected by the fact that over 80% of the initiatives are driven by opportunity rather than necessity. These facts strongly suggest that Australia is a place with business opportunities and individuals with entrepreneurial skills. This could be attributed to many underlying factors, such as social structure and aspirations and the high visibility of entrepreneurial behavior in the media. This attention and the role-modeling it promotes acts as inspiration for incubating entrepreneurs and is strong enough to push them over to become novice entrepreneurs.

It's also of interest that the internal market is the main contributor to entrepreneurial growth, as only 12% of the entrepreneurs aim at a substantial share of customers from the international market. One explanation for such an outlook could be the fact that Australia is geographically isolated from international markets, although with the advent of the Internet one should be able to see the trend changing.

Entry to entrepreneurship, while low in young adults (below 25), picks up for mid-career individuals, indicating a time lag in the acquisition of skills, resources and experience to considering the move. Past the age of 25 the rate of engagement remains high, even up to the age of 54. This is a surprising and welcome event for Australia as it shows low age discrimination with respect to entrepreneurial pursuits. Regarding gender, over 8% of the female population displays entrepreneurial behavior, again putting Australia second among the advanced economies.

Australia's entrepreneurship profile is what one would expect in innovation-driven societies, with 34% of them involved in consumer-oriented businesses and 31% involved in business services. The institutional conditions in Australia are highly supportive of entrepreneurs and this is expressed through entrepreneurship education, cultural support and the openness of its internal market. The country also supports an inclusive environment with no gender or age bias, which is highly conductive to entrepreneurship. The spirit of innovation spills over to other categories of entrepreneurs, such as employees in organizations, who are often involved and lead such initiatives.

Despite the positives for entrepreneurs, Australia also has a high rate of exit (31%), which could reflect a high rate of failure. While some of the discontinuations could be positive (a business is sold, for example), it indicates that there is room for improvement, either by preparing entrepreneurs to deal with and learn from the failure or adapt policies to provide better support. Spreading entrepreneurship to all the industries and enforcing it in all levels of private and public sectors is also a direction for the government and its policy-makers.

DENMARK

Denmark is a society that blends modernism and collectivism in a unique way and was recently named the happiest country in the world (2013). Individualism has increased in value over time, placing the country above the average in the group of developed countries, in correlation with an increase in the esteem of the entrepreneurial vocation. In general, the country seems to be progressing towards an entrepreneurial culture and engagement in entrepreneurial ventures has even been sustained during the current economic crisis.

Entrepreneurial education in the country is quite extensive, showing the emphasis the country is placing on stimulating entrepreneurship and the acquisition of skills. The government has also been establishing favorable policies and developing public programs to increase the pervasiveness of entrepreneurship. This is also an outcome of the fact that Denmark is a welfare society that extends its support to public programs for private business.

The availability of high-quality services in support of entrepreneurs (commercial, legal and professional) was on the increase up until 2006 but has been steadily decreasing since then. The same pattern is observed for the physical infrastructure of the country as well as for the establishment of private ownership of knowledge. Slow progress has also been made in opening up the market by easing market entry of new entrepreneurs, although it is still below the average of the developed countries. A lot of the slowdown that is mentioned here is an obvious effect of the world economic crisis and it is also reflected in the entrepreneurial opportunity space that has shrunk since then accordingly.

While the availability of funding has fluctuated over the years, the availability of resources in general seems to be declining since the economic recession began. Contrary to that is a steady increase in the exploitation of technological knowledge that public research institutions produce by entrepreneurs. National support for growth-entrepreneurship is on the increase in Denmark and is evident by the establishment of advisory services specifically targeting growth-oriented firms.

HONG KONG AND CHINA

Presenting Hong and China under the same grouping is a deliberate attempt to address entrepreneurial behavior of two similar cultural groups that evolved in different economic and political environments in the past. The comparison in effect will eliminate the influence of cultural stereotypes while attempting to show the impact and influence of political establishments on entrepreneurial behavior.

The city of Hong Kong is a particular case of an almost independent entity that was privileged in operating under a free market regime for most of its history. Despite this tradition, which was reflected in the more entrepreneurial culture one observes in Hong Kong, recent data indicate that only 3.6% of its adult residents engage in early-stage entrepreneurial activities, far lower than the almost 19% observed in mainland China. This is not unnatural since Hong Kong, with its Western exposure, was greatly affected by the financial crisis, while China remained unaffected, sustaining its growth rates.

The entrepreneurship behavior in Hong Kong seems to be strongly dominated by opportunity rather necessity, as those driven by opportunity were 2.6 times more prevalent than those driven by necessity. This was not the case in China, as the two categories claim equal numbers. Gender is strongly biased both in Hong Kong and China towards men. Women tend to become entrepreneurs from necessity rather than opportunity. Regarding age, the highest incidences of entrepreneurship occur in the 25–34 age group, with China again showing higher rates than Hong Kong. This analogy was maintained even in the older group of 55–64. The entrepreneurs tend to reach maturity and become successful towards younger ages (35–44) in China than in Hong Kong (45–54).

Education that in many cases is considered an influential factor appears to be of some significance to Hong Kong entrepreneurs, making a person with a postgraduate degree twice as likely to become an entrepreneur than an average person, while a person with only secondary education is about half as likely. The opposite is true for the rest of China, probably because educated people might get the better jobs, making risking in entrepreneurial ventures less attractive to engage.

The types of business entrepreneurs engage in in Hong Kong appear to be in both the services sector and in the transforming industries, while the opposite is true for China. This is probably due to the growth the mainland is experiencing in infrastructure as it tries to catch up with the rest of the world. Additionally, the mainland, due to the availability of natural resources, sees a lot of entrepreneurial growth in the extractive industries such as mining, forestry, agriculture and fishing. An interesting fact that has also been seen in other regions of the world was the unaffected rates of exits observed because of the economic crisis. Apparently entrepreneurs want to stand by and see what will emerge after the crisis goes in terms of expanding their business and exploiting new opportunities.

Hong Kong's status and history is one of the most stimulating factors for entrepreneurship there and is still triggered by the wealth of the city and its conspicuous Western-style culture. Its fast pace and international aura stand as a beacon of capitalism into the otherwise closed communist mainland China. Despite that, one sees on the opposite end a risk-averse society that values conservatism and professionalism over creativity, at least at the level of low-level entrepreneurship. This, as we will see in the following chapters, is the opposite of high-level entrepreneurship.

JAMAICA

Jamaica is an island country where entrepreneurial activity fluctuated over time, as a response mainly to the economic environment and the unemployment rates. The emphasis of the activity in both early-stage and established business is mainly in the consumer-oriented sectors (64% of the total), such as hotels, restaurants and retail trade. Other industries such as agriculture, forestry and fishing also attract entrepreneurs, although at lowers rates. Overall almost 14% of Jamaicans engage in entrepreneurship that is largely opportunity-driven. The two genders appear to be equally interested in entrepreneurship, with men having a steady marginal lead. A distinction in the preferences between genders appears to be due to the motive, as men seem to be driven more by opportunity while women are driven primarily by necessity. This is not surprising since women as the main caretakers are usually engaging in supplementing family income. This often also leads them to be involved in subsistence-type entrepreneurial activities.

Perceived opportunities, although generally in decline after the advent of the financial crisis, seem to be higher in underdeveloped countries compared with those with higher levels of development. The same goes for the perceived capabilities of entrepreneurs, resulting in high levels of self-confidence and low levels of fear of failure. This attitude could potentially be an asset for Jamaica and something the country might consider investing in heavily. Despite this positive outcome, the entrepreneurial intentions of Jamaicans were lower than the average for similar efficiency-driven economies, but almost twice as high as that of innovation-driven societies.

Becoming an entrepreneur is positively viewed in the Jamaican society and the greatest percentage of the adult population believes that successful entrepreneurship results in high-status individuals. This is interesting as in general the society doesn't really celebrate individual success achieved through personal efforts. It seems though that risk-taking, creativity and innovativeness involved in entrepreneurship are highly inspirational and appreciated. Entrepreneurs can be quite frustrated in such societies and the beginning is not well supported, while the successful ending can be greatly rewarded.

The government of the country, although it makes efforts to create an environment conducive to and supportive of entrepreneurs (by establishing incubators and government programs for new and growing business), is seen as ineffective in such a role as most households believe that the support for new and growing firms is not a priority for the government. Apparently it takes long to get the required permits and licenses to start a business and taxation and government regulations are not applied in a predictable and consistent way. This leads a lot of the small companies to avoid paying tax.

Regarding the commercial services and infrastructure in Jamaica, the majority of entrepreneurs believe that there is an adequate number of contractors, suppliers and consultants to support growing firms, but their cost is prohibitive. This is not true, though, for professional, legal and accounting services that seem to satisfy new and established entrepreneurs. The impressions of the banking services, on the other hand, fluctuate, making the ability to engage trained and skilful support difficult for new entrepreneurs.

SOUTH KOREA

Korea is usually classified as an innovation-driven economy that emphasizes services to address a growing wealthy society. While one would expect that entrepreneurial behavior might be higher in such societies, Koreans appear to score high in fear of failure and believe less in entrepreneurial opportunities. This has resulted in a decline in the confidence for start-up activities in the local economy and in the perception of the social status of entrepreneurs.

Despite these beliefs, though, a lack of overall job security had a positive effect on the intention of people to become entrepreneurs and subsequently has led to a high rate of start-up. A lot of these start-ups are in the form of experiments for entrepreneurs testing the waters and often lead to failures and business termination. Another reason for the higher rates for business discontinuation could be management issues that entrepreneurs face, such as low profitability and difficulties in financing the business.

The general infrastructure of the country and the support entrepreneurs receive are viewed positively by the majority of entrepreneurs, but there is a feeling that more support is needed in the areas of financial support, education, training, professional services and R&D transfer. The internal market dynamics are strong in the country, creating a conducive environment for entrepreneurship.

In general, the field of entrepreneurship in Korea is male-dominated and the more established entrepreneurs are in the 45–54 age group, with older ones coming next. Raising capital is difficult in Korea and a major source of financing for entrepreneurs is friends and family, who contribute up to 80% of the start-up finance. In spite of the rapid economic development the country has experienced over the last decades, the area of venture capitalists didn't grow much. This got worse after the venture bubble in 2000 and the economic crisis that followed, leading many venture capitalists in the country to become risk-averse. To address the issue, the government established funds in support of SMEs but the general impression is that more is needed.

MALAYSIA

Malaysia is an agricultural country where 60% of all companies operate as microenterprises, accounting for 30% of the non-government employment and totaling 6.5 million people. The majority of these low-level entrepreneurs in Malaysia operate very small-scale businesses, such as grocery stores, small agro-based production and distribution facilities, night market hawkers and food stalls among others. The reasons for engaging in such activities range from family tradition, survival, encouragement and assistance from the local governments, etc. The government made great efforts and invested heavily in supporting entrepreneurs but it wasn't successful in stimulating opportunity entrepreneurship. A great percentage of start-ups (90% by some accounts) failed within five years of corporation. The main reason identified was that although the start-ups experienced initial growth, they were unable to transition to managing a workforce and as a result missed market opportunities.

The government actually identified lack of basic business skills of entrepreneurs as the main source of failure, especially in properly handling the financial support they received.

NIGERIA

Nigeria's bad performance of formal institutions in supporting micro-entrepreneurs led a lot of them to follow informal finance avenues. This form of finance is predominantly in the form of cash transactions and while legal, it is nevertheless unregulated. Microenterprises tend to operate on small scale, keep few or no records and usually do not seek support from the government or public financial institutions. The entry rate to low-level entrepreneurship in Nigeria is much higher than most other countries, as the propensity for working individuals to leave their work and start their own business is high. This results in the loss of managerial talent for established corporations in favor of start-ups.

An interesting characteristic of low-level entrepreneurship in Nigeria as well as in the neighboring countries is that females seem to overtake males as micro-entrepreneurs. Although the available data are often not accurate, it seems that Sub-Saharan African women are quite entrepreneurial. In spite of their economic empowerment, though, their cultural orientation still considers the man as the decision-maker in the family. Another characteristic of women entrepreneurs is that they are savings-oriented, contrary to men, who are profit-oriented in the majority.

Age-wise, it seems that the average age of entrepreneurs is 43, with the majority of them having no higher education or formal training. Also the great majority of them (almost 90%) seem to operate within their local community and engage in more than one business activity. In fact, many of them exhibit quite intense entrepreneurial behavior and engage in multiple and diverse ventures (an average estimate of six businesses is normal). We could consider them ideal micro-multipreneurs.

Of course such an environment leads to a lot of copycat business (food stores, restaurants, auto repair, etc.) that, while one would expect this to undermine and demotivate newcomers, actually acts as an inflation controller and a harmonizer of functions. One of these is to rationalize tax expenditures and, in essence, invest profits in more businesses and another is to act as corporate treasury as the businesses can support each other in times of need. It's not rare in Nigeria to see a bank owning a variety of other businesses such as car lots, courier firms, sports clubs and educational institutions, all working and co-existing as one profitable group. This behavior is replicated at the level of the individual, making Nigeria the paradise of the micro-multirepreneur.

PAKISTAN

Pakistan has not been historically known for the entrepreneurial behavior of its people, at least from the official records' point of view. The country, though, has a large number of unregistered firms in its significant small-scale informal sector, primarily because of the complexities of the legal, tax and administrative environment. The areas covered by such firms include construction, transportation and communication, wholesale and retail trading, hotels and storage areas among others. These industries usually employ 80% of the non-agricultural labor force and the structure of many of these firms is that of sole proprietorship. Most of them are also considered family businesses.

Motivation behind engaging in entrepreneurship in Pakistanis is predominantly to increase income and, to a lesser degree, to acquire independence. The young and potential entrepreneurs find it difficult to start a business and even more difficult to grow it. Established businesses also report the same difficulties in addition to reduced business opportunities in the market. The society, though, highly respects successful entrepreneurs and this attitude motivates young people and especially males to engage in business formation. The female population intending to open up a business, although a quarter of the corresponding male population, seem to have less fear of failure than their male counterparts and are more aware of the status and stories of high-profile entrepreneurs.

Entrepreneurship was never really part of the focus of government planning compared at least with the focus and investment large industries received. The national policies and related support programs, including education on entrepreneurial skills and competencies, is considered weak, despite the fact that the physical infrastructure and market openness is perceived as adequate. The ongoing war-like environment, especially in the border areas with Afghanistan, and the security restrictions are partly to blame for some of the market limitations and the challenges that entrepreneurs face. Another suppressing factor is the regular natural disasters that strike the country, such as widespread floods and major earthquakes, that when coupled with the global economic crisis worsen the situation.

Scarcity of skilled labor and the reluctance of sole proprietors to develop professional management, along with lack of trust among the business community, are significant factors that restrict growth of microenterprises in Pakistan. The lack of trust is evident in many cases where entrepreneurs, in attempts to conceal information, might operate a business in one city and have bank accounts and mailing addresses in another. In addition, investing in employee training and hiring talent is seen with suspicion as in many cases talented employees will leave for better wages or to start their own business. Prejudice against the established is also strong, as many entrepreneurs believe bank financing is reserved for political reasons and other non-commercial reasons.

RUSSIA

Russia has seen tremendous change over the last two decades and that has greatly impacted the situation of small business enterprises. Their operation and development is directed by many new laws and decrees on economic activities in efforts to transition the country to a full market economy. The imposed changes, though, create a lot of confusion, primarily because the letter of the law is not clear, leaving room for different interpretations to tax and other officials to abuse and deter entrepreneurial behavior.

Despite these volatile conditions, individuals are setting up new enterprises. Unfortunately the statistics aren't clear enough as to what they represent. Russians can be abstract thinkers and comfortable with chaotic and contradictory positions and thinking. For the majority of entrepreneurs in the country, opening a business is a step to ensure income rather than to gain autonomy and become wealthy. Seeking a business opportunity is the motive behind the majority of early-stage entrepreneurs, although a lot of them are driven by external circumstances.

While the attraction of opening a business motivates the younger generations, the average age of potential entrepreneurs is 37. No significant gender differences are observed. The level of entrepreneurial intentions is relatively low but tends to increase after 2009 as the economic crisis kicked in and more people turned to entrepreneurship by necessity after being laid off. For some reason, though, the intentions did not materialize for many, keeping the growth of entrepreneurial activity low. This was also reflected in the low viability of businesses.

The educational demographics of early-stage and established entrepreneurs show a clear predominance (80%) of people with incomplete higher education or professional degrees. A great percentage, though, seems to consider knowledge and experience (even informal) as necessary for opening up a business. Education also inversely correlated with the fear of failure, giving the more educated a clear advantage in that area.

In 2011 Russia showed signs of exiting the crisis, leading a lot of entrepreneurial behavior to be opportunity-driven. The big cities offer the greatest opportunities for entrepreneurship as do the smaller rural localities. Weirdly enough, cities of around a million inhabitants, despite the fact that they have the infrastructure to support entrepreneurship and provide wider fields of opportunities, tend to pose the most challenges, primarily because of the psychological and motivational peculiarities of early-stage entrepreneurs.

Financing a business is mainly done through bank loans and support from friends and relatives, while informal capital is a consistent contributing source of finance. These informal investments come from the extended network of the entrepreneur and play an important role in the growth of Russian entrepreneurs. This form of financing differentiates informal non-entrepreneur investors, who tend to finance based on relations, from formal ones, who tend to finance based on the opportunity potential for success.

Regarding the sector preferences of Russian entrepreneurs, over 50% of them engage in the consumer sector, while less than 10% are involved in the services sector. This shows a weakness to compete in the knowledge and technology areas. Overall entrepreneurial activities show a positive balance sheet as the entry exceeds the exit. It also worth noting that exit in many cases (around 20%) doesn't relate with business failure and closure, but rather is an indicator of change of ownership. An interesting fact is that a good 22% of entrepreneurs own more than one business.

The Russian culture, primarily due to its recent political past, didn't support entrepreneurial behavior (in fact it was illegal to an extent). The inertia of the old regime is also evident in the education system, which doesn't appear to provide—at least at the secondary level—knowledge and skills necessary for engaging in business creation, and neither does it encourage sufficient creativity and self-sufficiency. In addition to that, the cost of entry into the market is high as the existing firms are highly competitive and the ineffective anti-monopoly legislation isn't enforced appropriately.

SINGAPORE

Contrary to a popular belief that Singaporeans are risk-averse, in recent years they seem (43%) to express moderate fear of failure compared with other countries. A good half of the population seems to consider entrepreneurship a good career choice and the majority considers that status goes along with entrepreneurial success. In general the culture values self-made individuals and emphasizes autonomy, personal initiative and self-sufficiency, consistent with the adopted meritocratic attitude of the society.

Despite the good predisposition toward entrepreneurship and the belief that the local market is open to newcomers, the people believed that the education system did not provide adequate support regarding knowledge and skill necessary to start and succeed in business. This attitude and belief is instrumental in whether people will engage in start-ups and seems to dominate their motivational factors. Singaporeans tend to engage in entrepreneurship after they gain some experience, as the average age at which they express entrepreneurial intentions is 35–44. Past that age group the intentions drop.

Despite reservations, new businesses have grown over the years in Singapore. Another positive observation is that new businesses seem to make heavy use of technology and rely on collaborations with other businesses, in essence relying on a local network of support. Regarding innovation and differentiation, early-stage businesses do not consider themselves as providing competitive products and services, at least with respect to other countries. The majority of these offerings, of course, target international customers, as one would expect given the limited size of the local market (in essence Singapore is a city-state).

The government of Singapore is extremely supportive of entrepreneurial ventures and this is evident in the respective government policies in areas such as taxes, licensing and regulations as well as the well-preserved and enhanced physical infrastructure it maintains. The conducive environment is also evident from the high level of funding made available by the government and private individuals. Still, entrepreneurs feel they would benefit from specialized business incubators and even better support for new businesses.

SOUTH AFRICA

South Africa has an efficiency-driven economy where the dynamics between supply and demand are relatively stable. This is considered as a suppressive factor (volatility is where opportunities lie) for the 19% of its adult population who seem to believe they have what it takes to become an entrepreneur. In that sense the country's rate of perceived opportunities is low with respect to other countries. Things look worse if we add to this the poor quality of education, which leads to skill deficiencies—that even in their elemental forms are vital for entrepreneurial problem-solving and planning. Women in South Africa are less likely to become entrepreneurs than men and, when it comes to race, Black Africans' intentions are much higher than the rest of the races (and especially the Whites).

About two-thirds of the people that become entrepreneurs in South Africa seem to be opportunity-driven, a trend that seems to follow the stable market environment of the country. This drive is also strong among Black Africans, who consistently seem to be engaged in opportunity-driven entrepreneurship. Women and Blacks seem to follow the opposite trend as most of them are driven to entrepreneurship by necessity.

Despite the overall attitude of society towards entrepreneurship, over 30% indicate that fear of failure is preventing them from engaging in entrepreneurship, leaving only 14% of the country's population seeking entrepreneurial opportunities. Apparently, the society is critical enough of failures that in combination with the strong belief that the government should provide, deters potential entrepreneurs from engaging in such activities. Additionally and driven by the fear of engagement, a lot of low-level entrepreneurs are running informal and survivalist businesses.

Moving from initiating a business to establishing one is another very crucial step and South Africa seems to lack the appropriate commercial and government support for establishing policies and programs that will open up its internal market. New and growing firms don't seem to be able to afford the cost of using sub-contractors and suppliers nor can they afford consultant support that is vital for supplementing the business skills and expertise of the entrepreneurs. Inadequate government investment in physical infrastructure, especially in the energy and transport sectors, and the ineffective operation and maintenance of the existing one makes things worse as it impedes the mobility of goods and services and increases the cost of doing business. Even the increase of the communications sector (especially the mobile services), which has one of the fastest growth rates, maintains that costs of the services it provides can be prohibitive for low-level entrepreneurs.

Regarding the labor market efficiency, South Africa ranks among the lowest ones, primarily because its restrictive labor regulations are heavily skewed towards the interests of employees, suppressing in this way entrepreneurial growth that relies on engaging talent and dismissing inefficient labor. The public sector also creates problems for entrepreneurs, as it imposes delays in the payment of suppliers and outsourcers due to its bureaucratic style and attitude. In a relatively closed market, for low-level entrepreneurs like the South African, the government's role in promoting entrepreneurship is pivotal. Market openness and the support of entrepreneurial behavior with policies and programs that people are aware of and can take advantage of will greatly boost the economy.

UNITED KINGDOM

In the UK microenterprises represent almost 95% of all business. This accounts for 4.5 million in total, of which over 75% are self-employed. With respect to the overall workforce, about a third is involved in microenterprises. A total of half a million new businesses are starting each year, primarily because the owners are seeking independence. The great majority of them were previously full-time employees.

Regarding familiarity with business ventures about a third of the newcomers didn't consult anyone and almost a fifth had just consulted people in their close environment. While some sought advice from accountants and banks, only 15% of them got professional advice from an official source such as a public agency. The demographics of the low-level entrepreneurs have a gender bias toward men and the most active age group in terms of engaging in entrepreneurship is 16–34 despite the fact that older groups dominate the field. Surprisingly 50% of the self-employed are above the age of 50 and are as effective as the younger entrepreneurs, signifying the aging population factor we mentioned at the beginning of the chapter. Surveys also revealed that more than a third supports their ventures from their own resources, while other popular sources of finance include bank loans and mortgaging homes.

An interesting factor about multipreneurs is that a third of the low-level entrepreneurs have been involved or continue to be involved in more than one venture. The great majority (almost 90%) of them started their businesses before the age of 44 and a fifth of the total even started their business before the age of 24. Fifty-five percent of them have university degrees, although they believe it doesn't add any value to their entrepreneurial behavior. Of related interest is that many mention Bill Gates (a university dropout) as a source of inspiration and role model.

UNITED STATES

The United States, like many of the "new" countries in the world, is a country that has been literally established by entrepreneurs. Owning a small business is probably one of the founding dreams that sustained its glory and appeal from the early days of the union to today. The scenario of owning a small business is so intrinsically appealing that 22 million Americans own a small business today. Yet the microenterprise field is relatively young, emerging over the last couple of decades as a way for minorities to engage in the economy and from the efforts of women's organizations that encouraged and supported female business ownership. A great influence and inspiration in the recent growth of the field was the online revolution, which, assisted by unemployment and the economic crisis, brought back the interest. We now see a lot of individuals venturing online.

The new developments in the marketplace have changed the traditional notion in the US that microenterprises and low-level entrepreneurs are in their majority minorities of different sorts and immigrants that in general have limited access to traditional credit and other services. The public and private organizations that supported entrepreneurs contributed to the growth by providing microenterprise programs that, in addition to providing small loans, deliver business training and technical assistance. Programs like these nowadays face continuous challenges mainly due to the volatile nature of today's economic environment. Key pressures come from the declining buying power of middle-class consumers (many of whom happen to also be unemployed), the aging of the population, increased outsourcing, the use of temporary workers, the decline of many rural communities and the growth of immigration.

While the programs adopted by the government and the states managed to a great extent to provide employment, their return on the investment is not appropriately studied. Additionally, they have failed to assist these enterprises to achieve self-sufficiency and sustainable growth. Also, the dependency on subsidizing the training and technical assistance services and the scarce resources have limited the support programs from scaling up to large numbers of micro-entrepreneurs.

The profiles of micro entrepreneurs in the US are revealed by the statistical data of the early years of the new millennium. About half of the microenterprises in existence had difficulty accessing bank financing. A little over 5 million of them were women-owned microenterprises and over 3 million of them were owned by individuals with disabilities. 650,000 were owned by African Americans, 800,000 were owned by Hispanics, 650,000 were owned by Asians and 170,000 were owned by Native Americans. Conversion data indicated that about 140,000 welfare recipients along with about 150,000 unemployed individuals would become self-employed. About a quarter of the total, though, was providing a low income for their owners.

The dominant form of support for the microenterprise industry in the US is business development services. Firm development at that level is not focused on microfinance contributions but rather emphasizes training and technical assistance. Although strategies may vary according to each organization, the main focus is on business-plan training and individual loans. This is accompanied by a wide range of offerings that depend on organizational capacity and client needs. Innovation is also a target and the objective behind a lot of the support given to microenterprises as it addresses the strategic need to reveal breakthroughs that can scale up to industrial levels.

The microenterprise field in the US has benefited from the lure of the entrepreneurial spirits of some of the pioneers and world-leading entrepreneurs whose stories remain a great source of inspiration for newcomers. The additional ability of the field to bring together social welfare and economic development has been identified by the government and the states, leading to the creation of support programs and the promotion of entrepreneurial behavior. It is strongly believed nowadays that low-income individuals can create businesses that become competitive and grow. Lending to emerging business coupled with sufficient other support can achieve high rates of repayment and lead to sustainable development.

Driven by the challenges of poverty and economic dislocation, individuals are drawn to self-employment and micro-entrepreneurship. Their endeavors offer value to society and provide political and economic stability to their nations as they reduce unemployment, they release the creative talents of everyone involved and they provide rewards and a source of purpose in addition to financial gains. While the concept of microenterprise is widely familiar to disadvantaged groups, such as ethnic and racial minorities, the disabled, women, the uneducated and low-income individuals, it is now spreading to non-traditional groups such as the over-50 population and the high-skilled educated engineers and scientists. These usually excluded individuals are given a chance through entrepreneurship to business ownership and wealth creation that revitalizes local economies in spite of the migration of major firms to low-cost countries.

Low-income individuals engage in low-level entrepreneurship in an attempt to create jobs for themselves and provide for their families. In doing so they also enrich their lives and balance demands between work and family in ways they can control. A lot of them even manage to create "high-performing" microenterprises that in addition provide employment for a small number of skilled and unskilled labor. Many others engage in entrepreneurship to supplement other income sources, acting in this way as a type of multipreneur.

In fact, the expression of multipreneurship (as we will also address in the following chapters) is stronger among low-level entrepreneurs than the high-profile ones. The reasons behind such distinction are easy to see and include among others the risk levels and the impact a failure that is proportionally more costly the higher the level of multipreneurship. The time and effort demand also grows as the size of the ventures increases because of the complexities that larger management teams introduce.

One theoretical perspective is that multipreneurs should be generalists, while employees need to be specialists. If that perspective is true, we should be able to observe different human capital investment patterns for each category. While there is anecdotal evidence to suggest such a position (for instance graduates of MBA programs with varied curriculums tend to be more entrepreneurial than others), additional findings indicate that especially in the case of multipreneurship this is more evident.

Chapter 4

High-profile Multipreneurs

Like every human endeavor, multipreneurship has its low-level contributors that form the mass of its existence, but also has the selected few that shine like rock stars and provide the inspiration and attraction of younger generations to the profession. These individuals become a brand by themselves and surpass the brand of the corporations they build, at least in the eyes of the public. Almost all of them went from "zero" to "hero" in a few decades, at times by capitalizing on their family wealth and resources, and at times by bringing together the talent and resources of others. These multipreneurs that engage in multibillion-dollar international enterprises are a category on their own and will be the focus of this chapter.

There are two ways an individual can achieve greatness in business: by creating or joining high power and status groups of other entrepreneurs and investors or by developing a hierarchy of command and control that would allow him to delegate power to efficient subordinates. The former case we will cover in the next chapter, while the latter will be presented here. Of course, there is a huge spectrum of in-between situations, but we will consider them in either the former or the latter cases, in fashion of residence of the popularity and media presence of the individual leader versus the corporation. For instance, in the case of Steve Jobs and Apple, the image of the leader as enabler and mediator of success is stronger than the image of the corporation, so we will present Apple through Steve Jobs. The opposite will be true for Jack Welch and General Electric. Although there might be objections to our classification, it is used here for convenience purposes rather than as an absolute distinction.

Considering multipreneurship from the engaged and controlling individual leader point of view, and given the cognitive load and time limitations of single human beings, one would expect successful entrepreneurs to structure their influence, or better, their command and control in a hierarchical structure that closely resembles a pyramidal one. While this might be true, at least from a visibility point of view, the ties that keep teams together and the distribution of authority and control, as well as the chain of ownership relations, are vital for sustaining such formations over time.

Of great importance here are the circumstances/context under which multipreneurship occurs and the processes used by entrepreneurs to develop their businesses. Spreading out to multiple and diverse ventures, while providing safety and assuring growth irrespective of crisis in particular industries, has many challenges. A major one is the significant administrative cost involved in establishing a separate entity. This includes the build-up of a new management team, separate financing and different operational environments. A trade-off between the cost of setting up a new business in a different industry and the cost of growing and expanding an existing unit (provided the market has room for expansion) needs to be made. This is in many cases, as we will see, driven by coincidence of an opportunity that appears before the multipreneur rather than actual long-term planning. The advantage for multipreneurs is that due to their previous and diverse exposure to successful ventures, they have a shorter gestation period when it comes to forming new ventures.

Setting up multinationals is a very challenging activity, as the calls for judgment are more frequent due to the volatility primarily of the international arena. Different markets around the world tend to be exposed to a variety of shocks, some of which cascade regionally and globally, affecting multinationals that by default have stakes in where the "action" takes place. The multipreneurs in such cases become easily overwhelmed and forced to delegate entrepreneurial discretion to their executives and proxies around the world. In this respect these middlemen need to act as entrepreneurs, and in essence become ones in their own right. What we observe is a downstream application of international strategies from the multipreneur to the managers of local and regional subsidiaries, and an upstream application of tactical pressures flowing in the opposite direction.

One way to explain the entrepreneur's development over time is to consider the various stages he is going through from conception to materialization of his ventures. While this will formally be the subject of Chapter 6, we will present here an abbreviated version of the structural process. For this purpose we will consider the entrepreneur as an individual that at the time of the conception of the business opportunity has developed and acquired, throughout his life, a set of necessary attributes. We are interested here in attributes that are specific to entrepreneurship and we will take it for granted that he either possesses technical skills and/or has strong aspirations in the area in which he plans to venture. In the next section we will highlight some of the traits one expects to see in a multipreneur, and hopefully these will be validated by the cases that

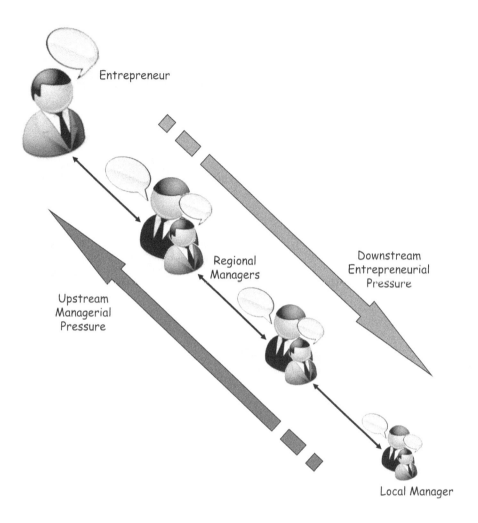

Figure 4.1   Managerial and leadership/entrepreneurial pressures

will follow afterwards. Figure 4.2 shows a representation of the entrepreneur with a set of unknown attributes on the left, and a hypothetical but realistic set of specific attributes on the right. The number of attributes might, in reality, be different, so in our case we use six just as a matter of representation.

In a more realistic representation, the lengths could represent the strength of these attributes, as can be seen in Figure 4.3, but for the purposes of our presentation in this chapter we will resume the structure of Figure 4.2. It's extremely difficult, anyway, to place values on attributes (despite the countless research publications that do exactly that), especially when used to

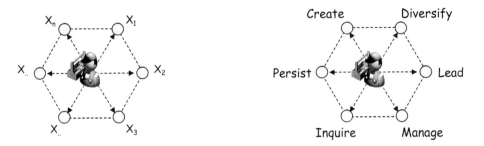

Figure 4.2   Attributes representation of an entrepreneur

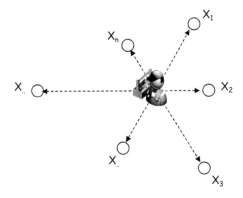

Figure 4.3   Weighted attributes representation of an entrepreneur

make comparisons between them because they don't have direct quantitative relationships between them—it's like comparing apples and oranges. The only reason we even mention it here is to show understanding for the familiar (and then reject it). In our representation, we consider that attributes are represented with the minimum required for successful venture formation.

The transition of an individual to entrepreneur starts with him as an incubating/nascent multipreneur (Figure 4.4) and, at least from the point of view of his attributes and skills, he is at the stage of a *specialist*. With this term we also consider strong interest in and understanding of a business field he might have acquired through formal or informal education and training. In our case of multipreneurs (Figure 4.5) we will consider that the individual has multiple skills or interests with prevalence given to the ones he displays and practices at the time of the venture formation. Many of the other skills might be hibernating, or displayed selectively and according to circumstances. One thing that we need to point out here is that the individual is already an entrepreneur and not an incubating entrepreneur by the simple fact that he already has and

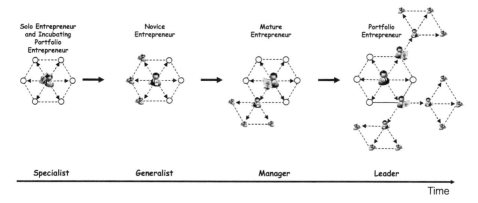

Figure 4.4   Transition to portfolio entrepreneur over time

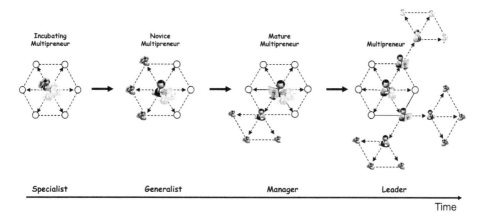

Figure 4.5   Transition to multipreneur over time

operates a business. Since we are interested here in multipreneurs, this first stage we consider as incubating from the multipreneurship point of view.

Fueled by motivation and engaging the proper attributes and resources, the entrepreneur starts his business, fulfilling by himself at that time many of its functions such as promotion, accounting, customer and supplier relations, etc. Alternatively, a small group of supporters/partners could be involved that might take up some of these functions. This initial core of people (if it exists) will be represented here under the entrepreneur label. An example of a business at this stage is a convenience store, a plumber, an electrician and a freelancer among others. It's a one-man show where all risk and decision-making are taken up by the entrepreneur, who is also reaping the full rewards of success.

As the business grows the entrepreneur hires more people and delegates functions that he was performing to them. At this stage many of the specialty issues become the responsibility of others and the entrepreneur has more time to work on higher-level issues such as critical decision-making, organizing the workload distribution and human resources. We might now say (Figures 4.4 and 4.5) he has transitioned from *specialist* to *generalist*. In the example of a convenience store, he is now hiring employees to take care of sales, suppliers and accounting, while he is more involved in expanding the business to other nearby locations and making it more competitive with respect to other stores, such as supermarkets. In essence, the business is now functioning like a mini-market. In the case of a plumber he might now have a couple of assistants and maybe a receptionist. He is delegating routine work to his assistants while still personally working on critical cases and outsourcing other functions such as accounting, for example.

The next step in the evolution will come when the business will grow enough to require a divisional structure. This is the case of a big supermarket with departments for HR, accounting, marketing, etc. Alternatively, it could be that the entrepreneur has expanded by replicating his business in a small scale, such as opening another mini-market in the same or nearby location. He is not any more involved in the specifics of his business functions since he delegated all that to others and is now literally a *manager* of people involved in high-level decision-making. The entrepreneur is now a delegator of authority and in essence manages people that act as his proxies in running local operations. His role is that of a pure *manager* and in the views of many the leader of the managers. He is now considered a mature entrepreneur and his additional duties now include planning strategies that will make his business more competitive and expanding further locally and within his national boundaries.

A final differentiating stage in the evolution of an entrepreneur comes when he manages to create and run multiple business entities that could either be replications of its existing business and their divisional structure in the same industry and in multiple locations locally and/or globally, or with the creation of new businesses in other industries. The former is the case of habitual entrepreneurs with a portfolio of businesses (Figure 4.4) while the latter is the case of the multipreneurs we are studying here (Figure 4.5). The individual is now an established entrepreneur and his main function is that of a *leader* rather than a *manager*.

This last stage is where the hibernating attributes and interests triggered by an opportunity and the safety of the established businesses will gain focus and be pursued by the entrepreneur. Venturing into a new territory requires heavy-duty involvement on the part of the entrepreneur as he will have to manage the requirements of the new venture that will include, amongst others, setting up a team, ensuring financial support, organizing the operations and establishing the business in the target market. Figure 4.6 shows this transitional phase where a new venture is sprouting from the attributes circle of the founding entrepreneur. The cognitive step required involves a tentative focused switch from the usual role of leading the existing business to managing the new venture. This is shown with the faded icons in Figure 4.6 to indicate the delegation of leadership functions to a proxy to lead the existing businesses and the assumption of the manager role by the entrepreneur to work on establishing the new venture. In essence, for the formation of the new business the entrepreneur is acting more as a project manager than anything else.

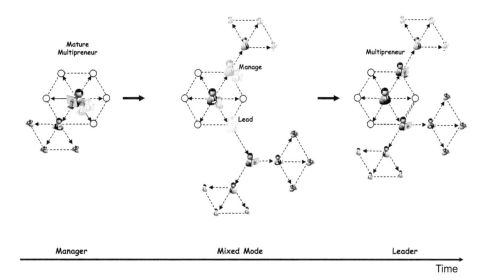

Figure 4.6   Interim step from entrepreneurship to multipreneurship

Having set up and operated two successful ventures in different industry fields, we can say the entrepreneur is now a mature multipreneur. Any new ventures he creates past this stage (Figure 4.7) will require repetition of things he has done before (at least in terms of the engagement of his attributes). If we wanted to identify this stage, we could say that he is now an established multipreneur comfortably moving between industries. If the diverse businesses he is building spread over his national borders, he has reached the ultimate "rock star" level, which is the subject of this chapter.

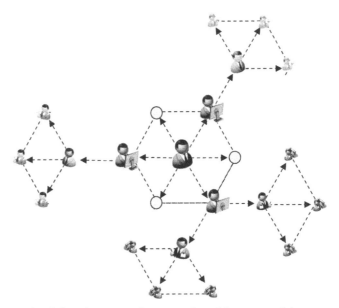

Figure 4.7   Final developmental stage of multipreneurship

The way we presented the multipreneurship case might dilute the initial notion of entrepreneurial core that we briefly stated at the beginning. We need to clarify here that by reference to entrepreneur we mean the entrepreneurial entity that grew over time. In that sense we often see a core of a few individuals that in the form of a partnership start the whole process, and elements of that core might even exist in one form or another in the final business structure (such as shareholders, executives or administrators). The role of these people is vital and was represented in the previous analysis in the form of attributes of the entrepreneurial entity. One of the partners, for example, might be focusing on the financial aspects while another might be focusing on product development and yet another one might be responsible for promotion and sales. Even in such cases, we presume here that the personality and attributes of a lead individual persist and to an extent overshadow, at least in the public's eyes, those of the other members.

To bring the importance of the team engagement into perspective, an interesting observation is that experienced and wealthy entrepreneurs value partnerships a lot more than novices and low-level entrepreneurs, who are more likely to manage the start-up process by themselves. One explanation might be that habitual entrepreneurs like to leverage their financial and professional resources and create more by spreading their investment and risk to more constituents, while at the same time taking advantage of the skills and expertise others provide. Having a dominant entrepreneur ("inspirator" we might say) makes a lot of sense in explaining the involvement of that single individual in multiple ventures. From that perspective assembling a team is of primary importance, as it literally enables multipreneurial behavior. Distributing the workload of a start-up not only alleviates the dominant entrepreneur from the full financial burden while providing additional skills, but also contributes to the alleviation of the cognitive load he would have to carry to perform the multitude of roles required to run many and diverse businesses. In simple terms there is only so much a "brain" can handle before overloading and making mistakes, so successful multipreneurs appear to have the wisdom to set up efficient teams and delegate control appropriately.

Experienced entrepreneurs have been heavily involved in businesses and during that time they have managed to build a network of collaborators and supporters that can later provide the resources they need to assemble successful management teams to pursue other ventures. A lot of those team members, as we will see later, are also entrepreneurs. For the case of multipreneurs that we are interested in here, many of those supporting entrepreneurs will come from the area the multipreneur is targeting, as he will need specialized knowledge and skills he doesn't yet have.

4.1   Personality Traits

Multipreneurs, as all human beings, display personality traits and characteristics specific to their activities. As we present the different multipreneurs we will try to highlight their personality traits that appear to influence the expression of multipreneurship. By personality traits here we mean the consistent patterns of thoughts, feelings or actions that distinguish one person from another. In more scientific terminology, traits are those internal characteristics that correspond to an extreme position on a behavioral dimension that tend to remain stable across an individual's lifespan. Another way of seeing them is as collections of psychic dispositions that give rise to a coherent, stable, consistent and predictable behavior across situations. Behavior in turn is what we see as intelligent action in the real world.

While there are many ways to measure personality traits, we will present here aspects of personality trait type indicators as a form of classifying personalities (Figure 4.8). Alternative theoretical approaches to personality theory include psychoanalytic, behaviorist and humanistic theories that for the most part deal with similar conceptions of personality. The indicators

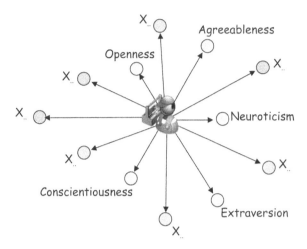

Figure 4.8   Personality traits representation

we will use here are rooted in psychology and are based in the notion that individuals have distinctive, unrelated tendencies to experience the world in particular ways that could be grouped in archetypal forms. One such sort of typology of personalities is based on five factors/dimensions (Big Five): *neuroticism, agreeableness, conscientiousness, extraversion* and *openness*. Similar scores on a given trait imply consistent reaction over time to the situation that triggered them. In this way we relate behavior to personality.

While these traits can be used to detect abnormal and potentially threatening situations, they also provide a framework for analyzing leaders' personalities, which suits our purposes here:

- *Neuroticism* as a domain comprises the facets of anxiety, hostility, depression, self-consciousness, vulnerability and impulsiveness, so in many cases it is also identified as negative emotionality or nervousness. Behaviorally it contrasts emotional stability and even-temperedness. The "good" aspect of it is when people accept the good and bad in their life patiently and without complaint or bragging. At its high end neuroticism is expressed with poor coping skills and reactions to misfortunes and life's challenges, while at its low end we find individuals with greater relationship satisfaction and those feeling committed to work.

- *Conscientiousness* refers to socially prescribed impulse control that is expressed in task- and goal-directed behavior, such as thinking before acting, delaying gratification, following norms and rules, and planning, organizing and prioritizing tasks. Behavioral examples of this type of person include those that arrive early or on time for appointments, study hard in order to be at the top of their class and look for perfection in their work. On the low end we find people with reckless behavior, abusing their bodies (substance abuse, poor eating and exercise habits) and people with attention-deficit/hyperactive disorders.

- *Extraversion* includes the facets of sociability, talkativeness, cheerfulness and optimism that jointly compose the higher-order dimension of "positive affect". People with this trait enjoy change and excitement in their lives and in general have a positive emotional predisposition about outcomes in activities in which they engage. The opposite is an introvert, who in general displays a negative valence mood about events and outcomes—termed also "negative affect". The level of this opposite represents one's level of subjective distress and dissatisfaction. High negative affect reflects a wide range of negative mood states, including fear, anger, sadness, guilt, contempt, disgust and self-dissatisfaction. In contrast, high positive affect is expressing enthusiasm, joy, energy, mental alertness and confidence.

- *Agreeableness* is best conceptualized as summarizing specific tendencies and behaviors such as being kind, considerate, likable, cooperative and helpful. Individual differences in agreeableness might be reflected as expressions of intimacy, union and solidarity in groups, where they can work as part of a motivational system. Biobehavioral research also suggests a link between childhood and differences in agreeableness and in particular as inhibitors of negative affect. At the high end, agreeableness indicates better performance in work groups, while the low end shows someone with interpersonal problems.

- *Openness* to experience/intellect includes facets of originality, complexity, aesthetics and values to a person's mental and experiential life. Openness is shown to be the trait that accounts for most individual differences in personality. Individuals with a high value of this trait are the ones that take the time to learn something new out of joy for learning and look for stimulating activities to break up routine. Artistic expressions and tendencies are attributed to openness as well as long-term education and research. At the low end we find conservative attitudes and preferences in politics, social behavior and towards life in general.

Regarding the multipreneurs that we study here, there are bound to be certain trait preferences that prevail and consistently characterize them. As people who accept challenges they would normally be found towards the lower end of the neuroticism trait, while regarding extraversion they should probably be found at the high end, primarily because of their continuous engagement in diverse groups such as their teams, partners, suppliers and customers in their multiple ventures. Multipreneurs also by nature of their engagement in diversified activities will be expected to be found at the high end of the openness trait. Regarding the agreeableness trait, we should expect to see them also towards the high end as they are good and effective group leaders. The last trait, conscientiousness, might prove to be something of a challenge trait for multipreneurs, but with preference towards the lower end as they appear to not always be good at impulse control and constraining from risk.

4.2   Selected Cases of High-profile Multipreneurs

Similar to the previous chapter, where we discussed the cultural elements of low-level entrepreneurship by presenting its appearance and current status through cases of countries from around the world, in this section we will give the brief story behind high-profile multipreneurs (presented in alphabetical order). The classification, as we mentioned before, is mainly due to the media exposure and attention they receive. The list is indicative and covers different geographical areas, but in no way is it representative of everything that is out there. Important conclusions will be able to be drawn, though, which will provide valuable insight for the theoretical framework we will develop in Chapter 6.

ALHAJI ALIKO DANGOTE

The highest-ranked Black billionaire listed in the 2013 Forbes Billionaires list was the Nigerian-born Aliko Dangote. He was born in 1957 in northern Nigeria into a wealthy business family that provided for his education and initial funding for his business ventures. At the age of 21 he started his entrepreneurial career trading commodities and building material in Kano, Nigeria. In the 1980s he moved his operations to Lagos and, after expanding into his country, he moved on to take over the neighboring countries.

It is widely mentioned that after the Nigerian civil war Dangote modeled his enterprise according to the Brazilian model, complementing his trading company with manufacturing as its core business. His business portfolio includes food processing units, freight and cement manufacturing as its core revenue stream. His conglomerate dominates his local market in sugar production, while being the biggest supplier of soft drink companies, confectioners and breweries. In addition, his group is a major exporter of cotton, cashew nuts and cocoa to several countries. Further branching expanded the group into real estate, banking, transport and logistics, textiles and oil and gas.

The cement industry is probably his greatest asset as it holds the number one position in Africa. It is also involved in telecommunications, building fiber optic cables for Nigeria. His strategy was to set himself apart from the competition, building a strong brand that would be associated with quality. Another goal was to set up a strong distribution network that will ensure delivery of his goods as fast as possible at the lowest possible cost while maintaining a uniform price across territories. The internationalization efforts of the group led to ventures in Malaysia, Tanzania and Ethiopia, among others. Dangote Group is the only manufacturing company in Nigeria that has a presence in 14 African countries.

Dangote is the kind of person that is always on the lookout for opportunities and in many cases he leads at least at the country level. His success is attributed to his good start and the build-up of a network of corporate and political influencers, including Nigeria's ex-president Olusegun Obasanjo, which ensured him a virtual monopoly over much of Nigeria's commodities. Influencing the right people is one of his key achievements, as he has occasionally stated.

Aliko Dangote's success can be attributed to both personal and social traits and a strong belief in the image he projects to the world. As he states, passion and determination are absolutely necessary for building a successful business. These qualities can help one endure the challenges of the competitive business world while feeling rewarded. Having a sense of purpose in life is one of the greatest drives for a multipreneur like Dangote. For him it is important how he will be remembered after his death, so leaving behind him a legacy as Africa's greatest industrialist has been a strong drive.

CARLOS SLIM HELU

Carlos Slim Helu was the son of a Lebanese immigrant shopkeeper in Mexico City who managed to reach to the top of the wealthiest persons in the 21st annual Forbes Billionaires list. His holdings span many industries such as telecoms, banking, energy, tobacco and more. He is well known for his passion for baseball, the fact that he doesn't use a computer and his strong capacity to remember details in his head.

Early in his life Slim was exposed by his father to money thinking by giving him an allowance and requiring him to keep track of his spending. Education wise, he got a degree in engineering while teaching math for money during his college years. His business education was informal and can be mainly attributed to the lessons his father taught him and the influence he exerted on young Slim. All of his life Slim would recall his father's request to keep records of his expenses with the allowance he was getting as a little boy.

During the 1910 revolution his father started acquiring real estate, a trait he picked up and continued further with his early fortune. By the age of 26 Slim had accumulated almost a quarter of a million dollars through investments and inheritance which he dedicated into making profit. In the 1960s Slim showed his multipreneurial skills by buying a bottling plant and creating a real estate and a construction company. His conglomerate was named Grupo Carso and a decade later bought the Cigatam cigarette company. In 1982 and in the midst of the economic collapse of Mexico, Slim invested heavily in suffering Mexican companies, a move that paid multifold during the recovery times. In that wave of investments he bought an insurance company that brought him a return of 100 times and a retail chain whose value increased by almost 20 times. These acquisitions were followed by an auto parts manufacturing company, a mining company and much more, bringing the overall worth of Grupo Carso to $8 billion a few years ago.

All of this activity was kept away from the media and the public up until the time he entered the telecom sector in 1990 with the acquisition of the then state-owned phone company. It was widely speculated that his influence and support of the ruling party at the time ensured his success in the bid. Part of the privatization incentives of the deal was an ensured monopoly for the first seven years, allowing Slim to charge high prices while tripling the market size.

With the doubling of his business from the telecom company, he ventured into the wireless business, also taking the lead in this sector.

Expanding his reach into the rest of the continent was a natural step for Slim and was achieved by acquiring wireless assets from AT&T and Verizon during the dot-com bust. His cell phone company America Movil was estimated to have 124 million customers in more than a dozen Latin American nations. Strong connections with government officials were an asset for Slim, allowing him to gain glamorous government contracts that resulted in excessive profits. Towards the end of his business career Slim started delegating control to his children and their spouses and turned into a philanthropist.

Slim valued the family idea tremendously and was relying on their support to run and establish his businesses. The trust he extended to them and his executive team of confidantes allowed him to concentrate his efforts on expanding his business within divergent industries. His strategy all along was that of cheap acquisitions, followed by investing energy and money into turning them profitable and driving competitors out of business as aggressively as needed. His drive was always the establishment of a monopoly of some sort that would allow him to profit from higher prices. Despite his great success, he restrained from the typical flamboyant lifestyle of other Latin American billionaires and kept a modest profile. He was always very private, an insomniac (as written in the press) who enjoyed reading history—his favorite role model being Genghis Khan and his deceptive strategies.

ELON MUSK

Born in South Africa, Elon Musk is probably the "geekiest" of modern entrepreneurs, to use the slang term for technology entrepreneurs. The son of an engineer and a nutritionist and author mother, he taught himself computer programming early on and developed a computer program that he sold for $500. He moved to Canada when he was 17 in an attempt to avoid serving in the South African army. He then moved to the US to seek his fortune in the most entrepreneurial market in the world. He pursued his education and got degrees in physics and business. Following that, he pursued a PhD in applied physics and material sciences at Stanford, but his entrepreneurial aspirations had another path planned for his future.

He soon dropped out of school to create with his brother his first start-up, Zip2. This was a website that provided content publishing software for various news organizations. Their customers included some well-known organizations such as the *New York Times* and HEARST Corporation, among others. Working up to 100 hours per week he managed to ensure the success of his business, which he later sold for over $300 million, making him a millionaire at the age of 28.

With the profits he made, Elon created PayPal, offering online financial services and email payments. After an initial public offering, the company was bought out by eBay (rather unwillingly). Following some of his childhood fantasies, Elon decided to move into the space industry and literally compete with NASA in space technology by forming the SpaceX company. He started the venture all alone, investing almost his full net worth at the time.

The risk paid off and in 2009 the company became the first to launch a privately funded liquid-fuelled rocket into space and put a satellite into orbit. This was followed by the 2012 launch of the SpaceX Dragon vehicle, which successfully docked with the International Space Station. This was another first for a commercial company and established SpaceX as a mature space company. His software knowledge came into action when he led a team in his company to develop software for designing rocket parts by hand movement through the air.

In parallel with his space venture, Elon invested in building the first fully electric production sports car with the creation of Tesla Motors. The company produced the Tesla Roadster and has proven to be a great success. This allowed the company to produce a more affordable model for the public with a hybrid option for gas engine. The success was not easy, though, as the company ran into financial difficulties due to the high cost of the end products, leading Elon to personally take over as CEO. The comeback was outstanding, resulting in $70 million profits.

Elon was also involved in another venture at the time, SolarCity, which was developing solar power systems. With all three ventures growing and trying to reach maturity at the same time, Elon can probably be seen as the top start-up multipreneur. This situation was far from easy as capital issues that many start-ups face hit him. The fact that none of his companies at the time was mature enough to support the others forced him to lay off staff and shrink his operations. To the surprise of most observers and the public, he managed to pull through and even got a $1.6 billion contract with NASA. SolarCity also became that largest provider of solar power systems in the US.

As an entrepreneur, Elon is quite ruthless when taking risks, in the sense that he doesn't mind throwing everything he has (materially and emotionally) into something that excites him and that he believes has potential for success. He is more of the renaissance type of personality, engaging in many of the arts and crafts of his time. He was faced with a lot of suspicion and doubt as he challenged traditional industries such as the automobile industry, but one would say he literally took them by surprise, as most were rather inactive to his threat to react seriously, betting heavily on his failure. It's a clear case where the will and wits of the individual challenge a sluggish establishment and change it.

Elon seems like he came out of science fiction (a technological wizard of some sort), as if he fell off a spaceship now pushing humanity to reach the levels that technology now affords. It is a rare case of a young life with big dreams and ambitions that came true so fast. This, though, is by no means an accident. It is a testament to his vision, passion, dedication, hard work and a great dose of good old talent.

LI KA-SHING

Li was a native Chinese who at the beginning of World War II fled to Hong Kong with his family. His father was a teacher and he himself was a bright and avid student with curiosity about the world around him. As a young child he was impressed by the need to be ambitious and hard-working and endure the hardships of life. The economy during those times was in bad shape and Li was employed in a variety of jobs. Things got better after the end of the War when the British colonial rule was established, again providing the stability required for commerce to flourish.

His first entry into the business world was as a salesman in a post-war factory of belts and watchbands. Noticing that a lot of the entrepreneurs of his time started from sales, he invested in building a network of associates and business clients, capitalizing on his innate ability in building relationships. Along the way he gained a reputation as a hard-working and intelligent employee. He was also a strong believer in education and he would supplement his 16-hour work day with tutorials that helped him finish high school. Early on he realized the importance of communication through the English language and he taught himself the language. All of his efforts resulted in him getting the general manager's position at the factory at the age of 20.

With the administrative and business experience he gained and with capital from his savings and loans from friends and relatives, he decided to venture by himself into manufacturing. His first products were small plastic combs and soapboxes. Gradually he increased his offerings to include plastic toys for children for the local Hong Kong and China markets. While his plastics company was experiencing steady growth, the Korean War brought economic embargos that heavily limited the market option for any Hong Kong business. Despite the embargo, his company was one of the few that survived the depression and easily bounced back with a very successful novelty item, plastic flowers.

While his success in the field was cemented with deals from the US, Li was on the lookout to diversify his business by moving into land ownership for commercial development. At that time the political climate in China did not favor business in Hong Kong, resulting in a lot of businessmen moving out, which led to a drop in real estate prices. Li saw that as an opportunity and acquired many prime locations that he later sold at high prices. In 1975 Li moved into financial services with an international partnership with a Canadian bank. This enabled him to invest more in real estate and acquire hotels in Hong Kong and abroad, raising him to millionaire status.

Following that success, Li acquired the first British-owned firm Hutchison Whampoa, a first fit of its kind by a Chinese. The deal was executed quickly and quietly without anyone else able to access the majority shares he acquired. While diversifying Li didn't lose interest in his existing business and expanded his real estate activities to major holdings in Canada. This was achieved with the help of past associates and his influence in the banking sector. An additional acquisition in Canada was Husky Oil, allowing him entry into the oil business.

Further diversification came with entry into the cellular phone business in 1985. Although the business was doing really badly at the beginning, Li took it upon himself to promote it. A classic move was to hold one mobile in his hand while bidding and make a phone call. When a status symbol like him was role-modeling something, it was bound to be replicated by many, so his mobile business took off, capturing half of the new market. Moving into the television business soon followed with direct broadcast satellite, whereby he purchased the Westar VI satellite. This engagement allowed him to widen his geographical reach to 2.7 billion people all over Asia. The success of his new venture gave him the nickname of "Mr. Money", a promotion from his initial one of "The King of Plastics".

A latest engagement for Li was in the development of ports and shipping in Hong Kong and China, a vital component for his supply chain of the products and services his various businesses needed. By 1991 Li controlled 63% of Kwai Chung's shipping capacity and also acquired the Felixstowe Dock and Railway Company in England's largest container port. This was followed with investments for developing ports in China.

Li's involvement at the end of his career included a portfolio of a diverse group of companies. Despite his raised status, Li's philosophy always remained one of respecting others and never taking advantage of anyone. His success was always based on loyalties that he extended to friends and associates and the benefits he gained in return from them. Of special influence to Li's deal-making capability was the connections he cherished with mainland China. Building trust was, according to him, the hallmark of his success and one of his most important assets. Li wouldn't miss out on opportunities for growth and diversification and in that sense he is the ultimate multipreneur, at least in the list of cases we present here.

RICHARD BRANSON

Sir Richard Branson was born in 1950 in England, the grandson of a judge, the son of a barrister and of a most adventurous mother, who was a pilot trainer during World War II, ballet dancer and stewardess afterwards. Running a real estate business and serving as a military police officer, probation officer and novelist at times, his mother would continually set challenges (mainly physical) for him and one can only wonder if Richard inherited a lot of her personality. Being dyslexic and stuttering, Richard had a poor academic performance in school and—given that no one at the time knew about such disabilities—he was often classified as lazy and "slow". He compensated well by being intuitive, open-minded and risk-taking—even fearless at times—and with excellent performance in physical activities, something that he kept displaying throughout his life. In addition to making him quite forthcoming when interacting with others, his family's support was also a great boost for his confidence and made him quite persistent in his endeavors.

Richard eventually dropped out of school and went into publishing the *Student Magazine*. The magazine was not very successful but he discovered a way to make money by advertising popular records through it, eventually leading to the creation of Virgin Records. He opened up his first record store in Oxford Street in London and its hippy-like style made it a huge success, leading eventually to its replication all over the world and establishing it as one of the leading record labels in the world. He then moved into producing with signing controversial but popular bands such as the Sex Pistols and Culture Club in the late 1970s and early 1980s.

In 1984—and out of the blue—Branson launched Virgin Atlantic Airways, a shocking move by many, as the music and airline industries had nothing in common. Despite the predictions for failure, the company made it through although at a difficult time Branson was forced to sell his record label to EMI for $1 billion to support it. Afterwards, though, he created V2 Records to re-enter the music industry. Virgin Atlantic Airways is a worldwide airline now with bases in the US and Australia and collaborations with major airlines such as Singapore Airlines and Delta.

In 1985, following the successful launch of his airline, Branson opened up Virgin Holidays. While the company was initially set up to provide services for the airline, it soon became one of the largest and most successful long-haul holiday operators in the UK.

The transportation profile of Branson was enhanced in 1997 with Virgin Trains and Virgin Rail, which provides long-distance passenger services serving a metropolitan population of over 18 million people.

In 1995 Branson ventured into the financial services industry with Virgin Money plc, a UK-based bank and financial services company. The company expanded its reach with the acquisitions of Church House Trust in 2010 and Northern Rock banks in 2012. Branson's diversification thirst (addiction, some would say) led him to launch Virgin Galactic in 2004 with the sole purpose of offering sub-orbital spaceflights. Future plans of the company include the offering of orbital human space flights as well.

Branson's additional ventures in the 1990s (not always successful) include Virgin Radio, Virgin Vodka, Virgin Cola, Virgin Brides (specializing in weddings and bridal wear), Virgin Vie (retailer and distributor of cosmetics), Virgin Active (chain of health clubs) and Virgin Mobile (wireless communications brand). In the 2000s new ventures included Virgin Healthcare (providing services to the National Health Service in England) and Virgin Media (providing fixed and mobile telephone, television and broadband Internet services). Recently (2010s), Branson launched Virgin Racing (a Formula One team) and Virgin Produced (a film, television and entertainment company based in Los Angeles).

Richard Branson is generally considered a transformational leader with a strong sense of social responsibility. This has been reflected in many humanitarian initiatives he undertook, such as the establishment of Virgin Fuel Fund in response to global warming with the sole purpose of developing and offering revolutionary, environmentally friendly and cheaper fuel for transportation. Another such initiative was the Virgin Earth Challenge, a $25 million prize for whoever can demonstrate a commercially viable design that will result in the steady removal of greenhouse gases from the Earth's atmosphere.

Sir Richard Branson is one of the world's most intriguing and successful multipreneurs. He is a highly intuitive, challenge-motivated multipreneur that has come a long way from a marginally performing student to become a famous billionaire with the glamour of a movie star. Raised in a stimulating environment, he became radical when it comes to venturing to new business territories and adopted a flamboyant marketing and personal style that always draws the attention of the media. Displaying unparalleled passion with courage and great networking skills, he acts as a role model for good leadership and management style who enjoys challenges in different aspects of life.

ROBERT KUOK

Robert Kuok is a Malaysian-Chinese tycoon who has diversified from a base of commodities trading into beverages, real estate, industrial manufacturing, investment and insurance, shipping and media. He is probably more known, though, for his Shangri-La chain of hotels. Robert was born in Malaysia from Chinese emigrants, he went to a private British-run school and he studied in Singapore, where he worked initially for Mitsubishi during World War II. After his moderately well-off father died, Robert and his brothers founded a company to trade rice, sugar and wheat flour.

Prominence came through the commodities trade and by the early 1970s he moved his headquarters to Singapore. He became known as the Sugar King, as he would occasionally control 10% of the world's sugar market. He expanded this line of work to include sugar plantations and refineries in Malaysia, dominating the domestic market. His close political connections with both the prime ministers of Singapore (an old classmate of his) and the prime minister of Malaysia allowed him to play a key role in the relationships between the two countries and ensure support for his businesses. A key ingredient in establishing this high-level support network in many countries was his willingness to partner with high-profile local businessmen and share the profits with them. These business relationships ensured the political support of the occasional governments, as he was also willing to prove his interest by appropriate investments in each country he was expanding. Kuok's networking and partnership strategy crossed almost any kind of political regime in the planet, allowing him to expand to Indonesia, the Philippines, Myanmar, Hong Kong and China.

With his early profits he was able to diversify into palm oil, chemicals, shipping, real estate and hotels throughout South-East Asia. In 1979 he moved his headquarters to Hong Kong for closer access to the Chinese market. He was now well known for his Shangri-La chain of hotels, almost 33 of them in operation at that time and covering the whole Asia-Pacific region by 2000. The luxury hotel chain was soon complemented with the more the affordable chain of Traders hotels. By 1995 Kuok also held private hotels across Fiji, Indonesia and the Philippines, which he eventually merged under the Shangri-La Asia brand. The same group also merged with another 13 hotel projects he privately owned in China.

Kuok is probably the most influential of Chinese billionaires in terms of the Chinese government and one of the first to make real money-making investments in the mainland. He was even one of the few businessmen who continued financing his investments (building the World Trade Centre), sustaining great losses at that time, even after the 1989 Tiananmen Square events when others were leaving. This was highly appreciated by the Chinese government, which supported him in return later on by allowing him a competitive advantage. This support came not only through licenses for the best locations for his hotels but also through inside support that helped him clear bureaucratic obstacles faster than any other businessman. Another result of the preference of the Beijing government towards Kuok was his selection as their advisor in issues relating to Hong Kong. In addition, the government appointed him shareholder and director of China International Trust and Investment Corporation, the Honk Kong-listed arm of the Beijing-based government agency to secure foreign investments. He was also selected to sit on the Preparatory Committee established to oversee the return of Hong Kong to China.

In 1993 Coca-Cola chose Kuok's company Kerry as its franchiser to mainland China, giving him a virtual distribution monopoly to over 1 billion consumers. At the same time Kuok entered the media industry with the acquisition of the largest English-language daily newspaper in Hong Kong, the *South China Morning Post*. He also became a major shareholder of the world's largest library of Chinese-language commercial programs, Television Broadcasting (TVB), and in 1996 took over control of the media conglomerate TVE with activities in film, music, magazines and books. In 2007 Kuok merged his plantations, edible oil and grains businesses with his Singapore-based Wilmar International, creating the world's biggest palm oil processor.

By using both private and public companies Kuok established an exchange network that blends money and risk. He establishes private companies to explore opportunities such as acquisition of real estate, minimizing the risk in this way to only the small private companies. When the risk pays off, these private companies are sold to the public ones and with the money he makes from the transaction he builds new private companies to explore other opportunities. In this way the big public companies, while they pay premium prices for acquiring the smaller ones, get them risk-free and make more in the long run. Capitalizing on politics and taking risks, Robert Kuok managed to build a conglomerate empire using an Asia-wide network of contacts. He intentionally keeps a low profile and operates as if he still owns a private company. He is very realistic about his business ventures as a source for profit and concludes that the secret of successful leadership is sharing the profits with your team.

STEVE JOBS

Steve Jobs was the co-founder and public face of Apple, probably the most popular technology company of the new millennium. Steve was adopted as an infant by Steven Paul Jobs, a Coast Guard veteran and machinist, and his wife Clara, an accountant. He was raised in Mountain View, San Francisco, at the heart of what would later become Silicon Valley. He occasionally pointed out how impressed he was by his father's focus on craftsmanship and fascination with perfection when he started assisting him from early on. Young Steve was also inspired by his father to do the same and learned a lot by watching him negotiate deals at the counter when they would go shopping for tools and supplies. He mainly attributed that to his father's good knowledge of the prices and the market and apparently he followed in his footsteps in his later dealings in the business world.

Steve was kind of a rebel in his youth—mainly due to his high intelligence and under the emotional burden of being abandoned by his natural parents—leading him to experiment with drugs and seeking the truth in Western philosophies while still engaging and exploring his engineering talent. It was the techno-hippie culture in California that gave birth to Silicon Valley and Steve was a proud child of that generation. The urge to seek purpose and direction in life led him to drop out of university and pursue his entrepreneurial aspirations.

In 1974, Steve took a position as a video game designer with the then famous computer game maker Atari. His love for electronics led him in 1976 (at the age of 21) to start Apple Computers with his friend Vosniak in Jobs's family garage. The funding for the venture came from selling his car and his friend selling his scientific calculator. The two literally revolutionized the computer industry by developing machines that were intuitive, user-friendly and accessible to everyday consumers. Troubles with Apple in 1985 forced Jobs to leave the company and form the NeXT hardware and software company.

The following year Jobs purchased Pixar Animation Studios with his own money. The company took some time to take off, but eventually became the leading animation producer with some of the most popular films ever produced, such as *Toy Story* and *Finding Nemo*. His initial investment of $50 million returned him $4 billion in 2006 when the studio merged with Disney. NeXt, on the other hand, was not so successful and he eventually sold it to Apple upon his return as Apple's CEO.

Apple at the time was still not doing well but Steve managed to revitalize it throughout the 1990s with products such as the iMac and iBook and brought it to the forefront of the industry as the most profitable company of its time. Under his leadership Apple's products became famous for their high quality and stylistic designs. In 2002 he launched the online store iTunes Music Store in the US after negotiating landmark deals with all major music labels, hitting 25 million downloads at the time. The success of the store was followed with the launch of the iPod, which instantly became a hit and raised Apple to the top as one of the most innovative companies in the world. By 2005 iTunes reached 500 million downloads, making it the most successful music store in the world. Along the way the computer product line of Apple was bringing out one success after another, culminating in the release of MacBook Pro and Apple TV.

The success continues with the venture into the mobile market with what is probably the most successful mobile device ever and one of the first smartphones without a keyboard, the iPhone. Future releases of the device kept firm with the success of the initial product. Additional improvements also led to the second-generation Apple TV. The pinnacle of success was eventually reached with the release of the iPad touch-screen tablet, giving Apple the lead over Microsoft at least by stock market value. Jobs eventually died in 2011 from pancreatic cancer, leaving behind him a legacy as one of the most impressive tech multipreneurs of all time.

The reason for including Jobs in our list here as multipreneur is not because of the diversity of the enterprises he built—since in essence they were all based on technology—but because of the application of the tools he developed, which are used in the information technology, mobile, media, music and entertainment industries, and the way they influenced and changed the way people communicate and work with computers. In essence, Jobs created industries where there were only products and he did that in the most aggressive way with disregard for the competition as though it didn't exist.

Steve Jobs was a master negotiator, insightful and creative with a strong sense of simplicity and aesthetics. The devices he created are some of the best examples of style, reflected in their shape, slimness and even packaging. You would buy a Mac Pro and it would be packaged in an elegant black box with a ribbon as if you were buying the latest fashion shirt by Armani. You were not only getting a piece of technology but an impression of excellence, a trademark of Steve Jobs.

4.3   Common Themes in High-profile Multipreneurs

The selected cases presented above are meant to bring out the unique and unifying themes (if any) that successful high-profile entrepreneurs share. Of course, delving into the personality characteristics of individuals is done mainly from anecdotal evidence and the subjective experiences of those involved with them. The results in this way can only be brief and qualitative accounts of their characteristics and traits that contributed to their multipreneurial behavior. Additionally, if we wanted to be more objective, we should have included an at least equal number of individuals who failed to become multipreneurs. Although this would have made it easier for the distinct characteristics of success to emerge, it would have taken the book in another direction, not to mention doubling its size.

Obvious multipreneurial traits that appear throughout the presentation include a drive to succeed, persistence, open-mindedness, hard work and engagement in entrepreneurial ventures from the beginning of their business career. The multitude and diversity of the deals multipreneurs made worldwide proves they are masterful negotiators, with a good sense of power and control. An exceptional characteristic is their ability to share their success, establishing in this way long-term partnerships, while projecting trust and commitment along the way.

Regarding diversification, we can identity two categories of multipreneur: one that treats diversified entities as just business opportunities and one that is more triggered towards the excitement of being involved in different entities. The former seems to be motivated from the joy and satisfaction of just doing business, while the latter seems to be drawn to the specific industries out of excitement about the subject and as a way of fulfillment of some kind of internal drive or dream. If we could classify them, we could say that one group is the purely professional as they are drawn to and enjoy the thrill of the money-making opportunity, while the others get a lot more joy from the subject/product they are after. One group is the professional money-maker and the other is the dreamer that is more driven by the creation of a unique specific product or service. It's unlikely, for example, that we would see Richard Branson involved in the sugar trade just as it would be unlikely to see Robert Kuok excited about sending rockets into space.

Another common characteristic that emerges is that successful multipreneurs are masterful executioners above and beyond all else. In usual business practices top management spends a lot of time speculating about the future, such as how the market will evolve and what segments are going to provide opportunities for profit. Based on that, they will then focus on what strategies (how) their corporations need to follow to adapt and respond to the challenges ahead. Finally, they will plan the tactical moves and changes that need to be implemented to achieve their strategic goals. This planning also involves who will lead the effort, what resources will be assigned and how they will monitor the process. Their job from then on is that of a relatively passive viewer, sort of like the general who gave the orders and expects to see what will happen.

This is where multipreneurs (at least the ones we presented here) seem to differ. While they will invest considerably in the planning phases we mentioned before, they will also take the lead in the follow-up execution phase and heavily engage in aspects of the new venture creation, especially where the action is. Another characteristic of high-profile multipreneurs is their ability to build great teams. They personally get involved in partnering and getting the best people for the job. By this we don't merely mean people with technical skills but those that in addition to technical skills have the right set of social skills that allow seamless communication throughout the team and with the multipreneur. Enabling people and making them feel they are part of something exciting and bigger than each one of them is a skill at which multipreneurs excel.

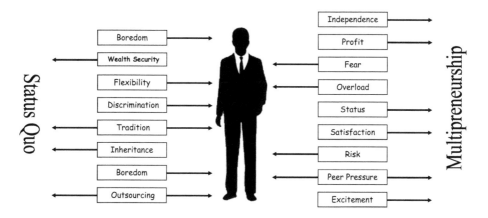

Figure 4.9   Pull and push drivers of high-profile multipreneurs

From the cases we presented here it appears that certain personality traits contribute to the expression of multipreneurship. Similar to Figure 3.1 in the previous chapter, we can represent in Figure 4.9 the forces that seem to act in turning someone into a multipreneur. There are forces that pull or push the entrepreneur and originate the sources of multipreneurship/diversification and status quo. A redefinition of *status quo* is required here as the situation is different now. In our case we deal with mature entrepreneurs that already enjoy success in their current business situation and decide to venture to new territories despite the "job" security they already enjoy.

A common trait of successful multipreneurs, as we've already mentioned, is that they are actively involved in the creation and follow-up operations of their business. This allows them to relate to each other by recognizing their achievements and respect their history in a way typical CEOs cannot achieve because of the tentative nature of their position. When multipreneurs speak, everyone else holds their breath because what they say goes. Their credibility is always a testament to their commitment.

Looking at the micro-social influences (the close family circle in Figure 2.9), a theme that emerges for many of them is the respect and admiration they seem to have for their parents, as they acknowledge the valuable lessons they took either directly or through role-modeling by their leading parent figure. Most of them had parents that displayed entrepreneurial traits or were stimulating enough to instill in their children a drive towards challenge that led them when they grew up to be motivated and persistent enough to pursue their endeavors and also get tremendous joy and satisfaction in doing so.

Trust in their child's ability to do well is also obvious, especially if someone delves into the detailed biographies of many of these multipreneurs. This trust was expressed by abundant support to their children financially and emotionally. Of interest also is that from early on a lot of those parents exposed their children to entrepreneurial aspects and inspired them to work hard for what they wanted to achieve. These "exercises" in will and drive might have provided the necessary cognitive skills they later needed to break tradition and venture where most people wouldn't, making them modern explorers in the market and the business world.

A surprising fact about many of the wealthiest multipreneurs is that they come from some of the poorest countries in the world, such as Mexico, Malaysia, Nigeria and China. It is interesting also to note that some of the superstar entrepreneurs never actually finished college. Education doesn't seem to be a defining influence in their success, although no one can doubt the level of intelligence required to achieve the feats they accomplished. Apparently being observant, open to experiences and learning from life can provide all the necessary lessons one needs for multipreneurial success. What education often seems to provide is domain skills that might lead someone to be more comfortable with certain products or services.

From the presentation here and the fact that high-profile multipreneurs can grow and flourish in almost any kind of political or economic environment, we can easily conclude that the ingredients of success (at least regarding our small sample here) are not to be found in the macro-environment but rather in micro-social factors that influenced their early lives. Serendipity and circumstantial factors will occasionally favor multipreneurs. But the adversities that our featured multipreneurs overcame is testimony to their ability to survive and excel, supporting the notion that these people would probably have flourished (maybe to a lesser degree) even if the circumstances were different.

Chapter 5
Organizational Multipreneurship

Corporate multipreneurs, although an unusual term, refers to those entrepreneurial employees and executives who are faced with the challenge of continually looking for opportunities and developing new ventures within their organizations. This is not an easy job, since pursuing new business ventures has to overcome organizational inertia grounded on established operational procedures and practices. Getting the approval and resources to start a risky venture is easier said than done. By their own nature the qualities of entrepreneurship and organization stand at opposite ends, as the first aims at disturbing the status quo while the second works to preserve it and make it more efficient. Finding the balance between the two is difficult as organizations tend to interpret their definitions differently and accordingly have different expectations of them.

While exploitation of opportunities is a primary activity of entrepreneurs, in the organizational context it tends to be associated with maximizing the output of processes and personnel by tapping into a surplus of unused competencies. It is mostly seen as adopting and applying practical methods and insights to release the full potential of the organization in a predictable way and achieve returns that can be easily assessed and evaluated. What resembles entrepreneurship in the corporate world is usually referred to as exploration and is mostly associated with experimenting with new options and testing alternatives with uncertain returns. The distinction affects strategy planning as it relies on different organizational principles.

The challenge for organizations is balancing the uncertainty of risk-taking with the familiarity of the established. This creates conflict among executives and managers, making it difficult for established firms to break through and remain competitive in volatile economic times. A way out could be identified if we focus on the way individuals and teams in organizations view and combine resources in innovative ways to produce something new. Pursuing opportunities within a corporate structure is usually more restrictive in the sense that organizations are microcosms of society with fewer resources available, but in another sense organizations can be better structured and are obviously more business-oriented than societies, so their mentality is more susceptible to entrepreneurship.

Having said that, we need to look at what organizational elements are fostering and supportive of entrepreneurial attitudes and which ones do not tolerate and suppress entrepreneurial (sometimes called intrapreneurial) behavior. Engaging in entrepreneurship is a strategic move for firms in order to leverage their resources to gain competitive advantage. Innovating in this way can have a positive impact on the growth and performance of a firm. The process creates new knowledge that the firm can further leverage to continue growing. In this way sustaining innovation becomes of primary importance to firms and is different from a simple strategy renewal or domain redefinition.

Some of the strategies firms adopted in the past to sustain innovation ranged from the adoption of entrepreneurial mindset, corporate venturing and corporate venture funds to bringing "Silicon Valley" inside. With the exception of the corporate venture funds, all other initiatives took place inside the firm. Internal entrepreneurship is usually of diffused intent since firms try to engage all of their constituents in displaying and engaging in the discovery and exploitation process of opportunities. Attempts in this direction range from being focused in certain departments or dispersed throughout the organization. The latter is an attempt to engage all employees in the organization and allow them to release their full managerial and entrepreneurial potential. The assumption here is that managers and employees can express simultaneously both exploitation and exploration capabilities. Enhancing one does not mean we have to suppress the other. Roles can also interchange as the conditions and the situations change, allowing the appropriate role to take over and address the issue at hand.

The form and design of the organization plays a vital role in allowing multiple expressions to coexist and take effect according to circumstances. Such forms at times might allow the dispersion of corporate entrepreneurship while at other times will inhibit their initiation and spread. An example of the influence of the form is a strictly hierarchical organization that is focused on exploitation. In such a case uncertain and risky initiatives that entrepreneurship brings are hostile environments for the administrative control systems. Another case is that of large bureaucracies geared towards preserving routines and procedures that are not susceptible to individual expressions of entrepreneurship. A way out in such cases is for organizations to build separate units, such as R&D, corporate venture capital funds and new business development, which shield these units against the negative impact and influence of the parent organization and allow them to fully adopt and function as entrepreneurial units. Separating from strong hierarchical controls allows for flexibility and organic growth, especially in cases where these units are small. Circulating employees throughout these units can further enhance their diversity and the potential to tap into the diverse employee base an organization might have. Corporate venturing provides an environment conducive to risky initiatives that diverge from the core business of an organization. Having small autonomous units responsible for innovation also benefits organizations in terms of economies of scale without compromising core functions. The units can draw resources and capital from the parent organization, benefiting in this way in terms of support and safety, while being free to pursue new and potentially high-growth opportunities.

Corporate venture funds have been mentioned here as a way for organizations to invest in start-ups with high growth potential that, when it materializes, can contribute to the growth of the parent company. Holding minority equity is enough to give an organization access to the discoveries and innovations of young firms without imposing on them the negative bureaucratic hierarchies of established organizations that impede decision-making and are consumed in political fights for power and control. Allowing start-ups independence enables their creativity and innovation to flourish under the control of the entrepreneurial team that created them. Of course, we also need to consider that not all initiatives will lead to success. Many corporate venture programs do not reach their objectives for a variety of reasons, which range from structural constraints to legal and political issues.

5.1 Dispersed and Focused Corporate Multipreneurship

Dispersing entrepreneurship in corporations and pursuing radical innovations can affect organizations in many ways. Research into the efforts of multinationals to tap into the unexplored potential of their employees led to the establishment of a number of mechanisms to seek and implement both exploration and exploitation of opportunities. Supporting an entrepreneurial culture across the organization seems to be the foremost important element in that direction. Allowing such a culture to coexist with the more traditional aspects of organizations requires alignment of administration and the chain of command stressing the emphasis on the exploitation of existing resources in creative ways that will produce new and alternative products and services.

Entrepreneurial organizational cultures are characterized by the degree of freedom they allow and the support they provide in pursuing new opportunities. Encouraging communication and information exchange is a major contributor to entrepreneurial behavior, as is the spirit and attitudes of executives and management that need to act as role models to stimulate intrapreneurship. The involvement of management in entrepreneurial initiatives is vital for role-modeling behavior. This display, though, needs to be controlled and balanced, as too much involvement might dominate the initiatives and suppress and deter employees from taking ownership of such behavior and displaying it themselves. In addition, too much involvement may project the impression that the manager is in control and aware of issues that would otherwise be brought to his attention, such as delays in project executions and difficulties in process execution. Research suggests that managers should be viewed more like coaches when they are trying to encourage entrepreneurial behavior, instead of taking active control and dominating the initiative.

Displaying commitment and support by top executives and managers can be achieved through the development of coaching programs that will spread the experience of senior managers to venture champions. These coaching activities can complement traditional roles of managers in entrepreneurial behavior, such as ratifying, recognizing and directing. Acting as part-time coaches, senior management can also provide access to their network of relations for entrepreneurial employees. In addition, coaching will allow management to control and balance the involvement of employees in exploitation and exploration activities without neglecting one over the other and making sure they address any organization needs and emergencies that might arise.

A distinction should be made here about the involvement in entrepreneurial activities of the various levels of management. Traditionally top management is viewed as responsible for entrepreneurial initiative, while the lower down the hierarchy one goes, the managerial responsibilities of exploitation dominate managers' time and efforts. In other terms, the top is focusing on strategy while the bottom's responsibility is in implementing the strategy and managing all aspects involved in its realization. In modern organizations, though, a bottom–up contribution to innovation is considered vital, as the lower levels are located closer to the technology and the markets in which the organization operates. In that sense, they can be more insightful as to what the current and future needs of the market will be and might be able to identify trends that top management cannot see, simply because they are not exposed to similar constituents of the market. The top would often act in isolation, more or less like a government that stopped listening to what its citizens need.

Allowing the knowledge traffic to the higher levels of the organization can provide top management with the insight they need for making sense of the environment and consider new innovations in their planning. Synthesizing the initiatives and recommendations of the bottom of the pyramid might seem like a normal thing to do, but it's a process forgotten in many large corporations.

Of additional concern regarding the initiatives of top management to trigger and institute entrepreneurial behavior is the way these are perceived by the potential intrapreneurs. Expressing entrepreneurial behavior seems to go beyond releasing personal entrepreneurial traits and is influenced by the self-efficacy beliefs of each individual. Gearing the support of top management towards the self-efficacy beliefs might be the way to go to enable intrapreneurship to be expressed and flourish. Perceived support and self-efficacy connect the macro and micro perspectives of potential intrapreneurs and in that sense they more completely explain enterprising individuals.

In the discussion up to now, we have purposely left the issue of failed innovation attempts. As research and practice suggests, tolerance to risk and failure is probably the most important characteristic of an entrepreneurial culture. While it is important to advertise stories of successful innovation initiatives and celebrate intrapreneurs on a regular basis as highly important for organizations, an equally amount of attention should be given to failures, especially as sources of learning. Perceiving failure as a form of "intelligent failure" adds value to those involved, contrary to ordinary failure where there is no willingness to assess and discuss the causes that led to the failure. Traditionally organizations have an anti-failure bias that predisposes them towards failure prevention. This attitude leads to risk-averse behavior and dictates conservatism, which acts as an inhibitor to innovation.

Because of such stances, entrepreneurial projects with relatively uncertain outcomes that could excite and get employees involved are not considered, leading to loss of talent who will seek to move to other organizations. The way out from such bias is a top–down wave of commitment to entrepreneurial strategies, support in the form of incentives and commitment of resources. Establishing appropriate policies might be a way to formalize the intentions of management and allow the entrepreneurial potential of employees to surface.

Another way to enable intrapreneurship is the focused corporate approach. The main issue with such an approach is the degree of separation between the standard operating procedures of an organization and the undertaken entrepreneurial initiatives, in relation to the benefits they provide to the parent organization. While having some degree of separation is beneficial for the expression of entrepreneurial behavior, moving too far and in extremes such as creating separate entities might end up isolating these entities from the organization and its interests. Additionally, while separate entrepreneurial units are flexible and free to act like start-ups, by being too far from the main organization and its competencies they are depriving themselves of their valuable resources, such as their existing knowledge base. If organizations are to follow the separation path, they must ensure there is adequate linking of the entrepreneurial units with the rest of the organization for the findings to diffuse and benefit the whole organization. This requires the adoption of a diffusion process focus whereby intrapreneurs are integrated with corporate managers to found and foster entrepreneurial ventures that can be subsequently integrated into production processes.

Some of the reasons why organizations might want to devote resources to the exploration and exploitation of opportunities through corporate venturing include financial gains from the return on the investment on new product development and alignment with the corporate culture of the parent organization. Corporate venture capital (CVC) programs can be considered a special case of multipreneuring. They are independent enough to be considered separate entities, allowing them to act with a start-up mentality and away from high-risk entrepreneurial activities and an emphasis on financial goals. Their use and value in the corporation varies and, among other things, includes the strategic objectives such as a better alternative to valuations and deals. Both the parent organization and CVCs benefit from efficient resource combinations and transfers, such as a knowledge-based perspective and infusion of social capital.

Mixing the financial and strategic objective has been shown to be the worst combination for CVCs. The complexity arises from the fact that, in essence, CVCs involve three interested parties in investment processes: the CVC unit, business units from the parent organization and the investment portfolio companies. Naturally they all want to benefit from the investment but their position and interests can create major obstacles. Failing to see the value of the portfolio companies is a major obstacle, which at times could be justified, especially when business unit managers from the parent organization have not been involved in the investment process from the beginning. Another reason for not leveraging the knowledge and expertise of the portfolio companies is the lack of commitment and incentives for the parent units. Formal commitment from the top management of the parent organization should be established and, with the projection of a long-term engagement, this would help alleviate this obstacle. Considering something as a short-term investment is bound to lower the interest in being involved in it, as the exposure risk could outweigh any benefits gained. Incentivizing can work well if the alignment of the parent business units and the portfolio companies is displayed and highlighted early on. In that case unit managers can see benefits from engaging in the interaction as it will help their units grow. An additional consideration that will help is to project an image for the CVC managers as brokers between the two other parts. In that sense their presence becomes less threatening and that of a mediating nature with minimum control over the other parties. Transferring knowledge and other resources will also add to the benefits of those involved if it is seen as a two-way process, with the portfolio businesses acting as entrepreneurial outbreaks of the parent business units, at least when there is an overlap of their respective market segments.

5.2   Corporate Multipreneurship Case Studies

Presenting selected companies as case studies is meant here to highlight some of the initiatives of these corporations that enabled them to display multipreneurial behavior. Some of them achieved this organically for some sectors and with acquisitions for others, while some focused mainly on mergers and acquisitions. Not all of the initiatives ended in success, but in following the success stream as we did in the previous sections, we will focus on the successful endeavors here. Following the objective of this book our rationale for including them will still be sector diversity as an indicator of multipreneurial behavior.

Another word for multipreneuring in the corporate world is diversification. This is mainly sought to balance the ups and down of the market in different areas. The rationale is simply that if one industry (say energy) is for some reason not doing well, the conglomerate can sustain losses until the sector recovers through earning in other industries (say healthcare) that might be doing better. In this way the survival of the corporation is independent of environmental pressures and can rely on internally controlled mechanisms (such as improving quality) to sustain itself.

One could write books about the initiatives that the select few companies we look at took as multipreneurs, but in the name of efficiency we will only highlight some of the more important that we believe contributed to their multipreneurial attitude and success. The companies are mentioned in strictly alphabetical order that is in no way related to their status or achievements.

BERKSHIRE HATHAWAY

Berkshire Hathaway is an American multinational holding company that oversees and manages a number of subsidiary companies. While the company started as a textile manufacturer, it later moved into insurance operations. From there and with the cash flow in advance of the payout of any insurance claims, the company was able to freely invest in various business sectors and expand its portfolio with acquisitions. The product and service areas it covers include insurance operations, manufactured housing, regulated gas and electric utilities, retail companies and wholesale distribution. International expansion followed with acquisition of metalworking companies in Israel. Overall the conglomerate now has over 223,000 employees in over 70 companies that it controls. It is also a shareholder in big corporations such as Coca-Cola, Wells-Fargo, American Express, Kraft, Wal-Mart Stores, Procter & Gamble, and many others.

The conglomerate is well known primarily because of its CEO, one of the richest men in the world, Warren E. Buffett. This is a well-founded reputation but to a great extent doesn't do justice to the organizational culture and the management that allowed this company to prosper, even in difficult economic times. Its operating structure is more of a model for extreme decentralization of operating authority and shift of decision-making into the hands of local managers. In this respect, the company's employees are the complete opposite of those from many of the big corporations that rely on strict control and oversight of regulatory compliance and management performance. There are only two main requirements for local managers: contribute with free cash flow to corporate headquarters and frequently submit financial statements. Apart from that, managers are not required to participate in investor relations meetings or with executives from headquarters, neither are they required to reveal their long-term operating and financial goals nor the strategy they will employ in achieving those goals.

The owner's investment philosophy is at the core of this conglomerate and it's based on discipline, patience and value. An interesting aspect of this philosophy is that it doesn't have intelligence as a basic ingredient. Ordinary people with skills and competencies and with the discipline to control their urges are what the company sought and in this spirit the company has never hired any consultant to help the executive team make decisions. Long-term goals is another aspect of the company's philosophy that is always abided by, seeking growth in small steps that last instead of going for what appeared popular and certain each time in the market. The company throughout time invested only in business with familiar processes and avoided unproven business models, especially those that came out of new technologies such as the Internet. It always focused on good overall economics instead of price competitiveness.

Berkshire Hathaway is an extreme case of diversification under the control of an influential individual and in a sense acts more as a venture capitalist firm than a corporation with the traditional sense of a strong hierarchical structure of command and control. Regardless of this behavior, the various entities are under the control of the corporate headquarters and in this sense the company is probably the ultimate multipreneur as it operates a huge number of diverse enterprises concurrently. It would be impossible for one person to be engaged in the management of all those companies. The strong influence of the owner Warren Buffett might lead readers to expect him to have been presented in the high-profile multipreneurs chapter, but his engagement is more in the way of a venture capitalist rather than a manager who is involved in the day-to-day planning of the companies he owns.

CHINA RESOURCES

China Resources is a conglomerate headquartered in Hong Kong and controlled by the Chinese government. Until the late 1970s the company was its main trading window with the outside world. It is now an efficient, publicly listed company spreading over eight economic sectors throughout China. Its main activities include: consumer goods, as the largest retail enterprise group in China and the number one chain of supermarkets; power, with investments in development, operation and management of thermal power, wind power, hydropower, coal and distribution-type energy projects; property, as one of the strongest comprehensive real estate developers in the Chinese mainland; cement, as one of the large-scale cement producers supported by the state; gas, by engaging in urban gas services closely related to everyday life, including piped gas, vehicle gas, distribution energy supply and sales of gas appliances; pharmaceuticals, as the premier pharmaceutical manufacturer and distributor in China; finance, by providing a comprehensive financial service platform, providing financial solutions to a great number of enterprises and individuals; microelectronics, as the leading analog semiconductor company in mainland China with a wide range of products; textiles, engaging mainly in the manufacturing, distribution and retail of cotton textiles, civil nylon silk, clothing, socks and leatherwear; chemicals, engaging in polyester production and liquid chemicals distribution and storage; and compressors for household, commercial use, air conditioning and refrigeration.

The company faced many challenges in its history but probably the greatest one was in transitioning from a state-owned enterprise mentality after the passing of Mao Zedong to instilling efficiency and productivity under modern management practices. While diversification was at the core of the company for most of its time, by 1996 management realized it was beyond its control and moved towards rationalizing its structure and streamlining its operations. As a result it closed several unprofitable or misaligned units around the world and in China while merging related subsidiaries and projects. Even those measures, though, didn't make an impact on its control and reporting structure, as many of its subsidiaries were not integrated in the corporate strategy and effectively acted as silos cut off from the rest of the organization. This was a general phenomenon as many companies those days were opportunity-driven, making it impossible to get a clear sense of direction for the conglomerate.

Shifting managerial focus from its profit centers to the overall well-being of the whole conglomerate was a major shift in its corporate strategy and one of the main goals of the then director and CFO Jiang Wei, who led the company to reduce the number of profit centers and reorient it around a growth strategy that focused on the population spread of the country. A result of this strategy, called "6s management" internally in the corporation, was a strong financial performance, with sales and operating profits increasing while facilitating at the same time the development of a strategy-driven culture throughout the corporation.

The "6s management" system comprised six interrelated elements of performance management that included budgeting, management reporting, internal audit, performance management, managerial appraisal and profit center coding. This was implemented across all the units of the corporation, including the headquarters group. The system remained as the core management system up to 2003 and was then replaced by the balanced scorecard and the profit center business strategy system.

The six elements address the following aspects of the organization:

- *Budgeting:* instead of profit centers providing high-level financial performance targets and operational targets related to volume and efficiency leading to small percentage improvements each year, profit center managers had to detail and rationalize their goals and strategy. This detailed budgeting process helped managers understand the operations of their profit centers better and expressed it in a common language for all centers. The budget targets of each center would then become key inputs in the corporate reporting system and would allow monitoring to detect potential problems and initiate countermeasures. Having the information on time, headquarters was able to decide on three- to five-year financial and strategic objectives and cascade down to the profit centers for implementation.

- *Profit center coding and profit center business strategy system:* profit centers were the result of regrouping the various multilateral entities the company had according to type of business and importance. A "tier-one" profit center was a grouping of similar businesses in each industry, while "tier-two" profit centers where defined at the industry level. It was a hierarchical system where headquarters was operating with "tier-two"/industries and each "tier-two" was operating "tier-ones".

- *Management reporting:* had the initial goal of learning about the operations and performance of profit centers through standard reporting formats. Apart from allowing uniform presentation of financial statements and easing processing and understanding of the position of each profit center, the new system was also intended to divert management from being dragged into speculation and to provide an opportunistic profit focus. This system, along with a demotivational compensation strategy for top management, was an attempt to minimize losses from short-term high-risk investments. Qualitative criteria were also part of the system and for tier-one profit centers would include customer satisfaction, new product development and brand-building, among others. The management reports would be reviewed monthly and the key performance indicators (KPIs) unique to each center would be studied.

- *Performance management:* different dimensions of the balanced scorecard such as financial, customer, internal process, and learning and growth performance were set in yearly "performance contracts" and would form the basis (70%) for bonus compensation for the managers.

- *Manager appraisal:* concurrently developed with the performance management system to capture the more qualitative aspect of the management teams. It would reflect compliance with the guiding principles and code of conduct of the company and would carry a 30% weight towards the annual bonus.

- *Internal audit:* implemented early on to ensure the truth and accuracy of management reporting. It focused on both financial and non-financial KPIs and compliance with the corporate culture and code of conduct. This also included examinations for deviations from the strategic plan of the corporation and was meant to prevent attempts at nonstrategic expansion and diversification.

By restructuring its organization and forming strategic alliances, joint ventures and other collaborative efforts, the company managed to grow over the years and become one of China's most respected and valued companies. Its primary goal that defines its strategy is to satisfy the future population growth of the most populous country in the world. This strategic objective would define the focus of the conglomerate towards consumption-oriented businesses that would be able to scale up with China's growing population. The company's acquisition strategy will also be influenced accordingly and as a result the conglomerate would target companies relevant to its existing profit centers, in a population-driven, high-growth sectors with high entry barriers and in industries strongly supported by government policies.

DASSAULT

Dassault Group is a family-owned French group of diverse subsidiaries. With its main interest holding in aviation, the company ventured in the design and manufacture of aerospace equipment, electric vehicles, software, print and online media, real estate, vineyards and art auctions. Some of the diversity stems from the general interests of the family that build the company, while other initiatives followed an expansion strategy to capitalize on the company's expertise and competencies.

Dassault started as an aircraft manufacturer from the early stages of aviation before the First World War and continues its presence to this day with both military and civil activities, holding the world's leading position in private jet manufacturing. Its engineering achievements led the company to innovate in 3D technology for the whole product lifecycle from design to manufacturing, by engaging communities of engineers and scientists acting in virtual 3D environments. The heavy investment in 3D technology paid off and a separate entity, Dassault Systems, was able to emerge and become one of the world leaders in 3D CAD/CAM (computer aided design/computer aided manufacturing) systems and whole product lifecycle management (PLM) solutions. The philosophy behind the success of the software venture for Dassault was its focus on the big issues their customers needed to solve, instead of their problems that usually drag development to specific needs and deprive them of the ability to evolve into something higher. The significance of the technological feat that such software can achieve is immense as one can have a team of even 4,000 engineers developing 1 million parts in virtual space and then assemble them to create a whole Boeing 777 on the screen in a perfect way and ready to roll into a prototype. Such development changed the face of modern engineering design and Dassault moved on by acquiring the low-end developer SolidWorks and became the world leader in PLM software.

The company multipreneured through acquisitions in areas far from its core business for a variety of reasons. It acquired a major French multimedia publisher, The Figaro Group, mainly as a status symbol and to leverage the image of the group. In addition to that it created a property company to enhance its portfolio and diversify further. One could say that the family would not be French without wine, so Dassault acquired and now successfully operates vineyards producing high-quality wine as well as divestment in a variety of vineyards across France. Another diverse venture included Artcurial, which includes a wide range of art and design business activities such as auctioning and bookshops among others.

The strength of the family ties and the personalities of its members are reflected in the diverse activities in which they are involved. To an outsider it looks like the variety of hobbies that different family members have, except in this case they all translate into multimillion-euro businesses. The values that made Dassault the diverse company it is today are passion, innovation, excellence and commitment. Going beyond the limits requires passion and in Dassault it drives their desire and enthusiasm to conceive and design original solutions. Along with the spirit of the aviation pioneers that founded the company, this multipreneurial company considers innovation as the merging of talents and skills. By investing in the collaborative capacity of the organization, the different businesses and professions of Dassault work in synergy.

GENERAL ELECTRIC

General Electric Company (GE) is probably the most impressive diversified technology and financial services company in the world. With products and services ranging from aircraft, marine and military engines, water processing, power generation and household appliances to medical imaging, consumer electronics, home improvement, and healthcare to mining, oil and gas to transportation and software, the company seems to be involved in almost everything. As a result of such involvement the company returned in 2012 the staggering amount of 12.4 billion dollars to its investors.

GE is the mammoth of the business world with over 300,000 employs in 130 countries worldwide, making it the kind of company that can shape some of the growth drivers in many market segments. The company is beyond reach in many respects, holding well over 20,000 patents and continually filing on average 5 patents per day. The expectations of creativity from all levels of employees created a risk-taking environment where employees are allowed to act as entrepreneurs and innovators. This is reflected, among others, in the way the company evaluates employees, as in addition to accomplishments it also considers their ability to reflect the company's guiding principles. These include: an external focus on collaboration with all stakeholders, such as customers, governments, regulators and the community; inclusiveness, such as breaking the barriers between team members and embracing diversity with respect and acceptance; expertise, such as deep understanding of subject matter and a wide knowledge base that is also able to be transmitted and developed in others; clear thinking as a result of decisiveness, agility and strategic commitment; and courage in releasing creativity. The capacity to take risk and learn in the process is inherent in these principles.

Investing heavily in research and development (R&D) globally enabled GE to continually innovate and keep its position as one of the world market leaders. It was a top–down approach, as the few CEOs that historically managed the company devoted a lot of time on new products, services and processes development. This trend started in the 1920s with rapid growth through patented inventions and product differentiation, even during the Depression. Later on, after World War II, the company decentralized its organization and adopted a diversification strategy with low production costs. In the 1950s it promoted a customization of products and services combined specific to client demand. Expanding into the 1960s the company moved into areas as varied as electronics, computers, chemicals, plastics, automation, power plants, nuclear technology and even space. More recent efforts in the 1990s changed the focus of the company from long-range product development projects to short product lifecycle development that allowed the company to market its products fast. This, combined with a streak of acquisitions and alliances, allowed the company to target local as well as emerging markets around the globe.

The spirit of innovation continues today with a 16 billion dollar investment in R&D between 2010 and 2012 in the midst of a worldwide economic crisis. Recent attempts to sustain the company's innovation momentum include its efforts in reverse innovation and open innovation as enablers of future growth. GE is a company that knows that innovation doesn't mean "jumps" and breakthroughs (although it has had its share of those), but it can very well come from many small incremental improvements. When the effects of innovation add up, the company is effectively raising the cost of entry for competitors that in addition allows the company time to experiment and venture into new directions. As one of its CEOs once said, "turning ideas into commercial reality requires persistence and discipline, and overall effectiveness ultimately depends on top management being able to find the right balance between corporate creativity and efficiency."

General Electric is trying hard these days to transform into a lean enterprise and eliminate the bureaucracy and arrogance that comes with size. To succeed the company is trying to infuse into its culture some of the entrepreneurial spirit of start-ups and venture capitalists. This means a shift in focus towards complexity, accountability and focus, as its CEO said in the 2012 annual report. Doing fewer things with bigger impact and taking ownership of decisions by being involved in the action is expected to simplify opportunity exploitation and the response rate of the company to the changing market landscape. The leadership movement nowadays is that of simplification. Using judgment, moving fast and being accountable are the drives behind future success. Accountability for outcomes is of most important value as it allows the company to compete with purpose and deliver outcomes for its customers, investors and the societies it serves.

GRUPO GARANTIA

Grupo Garantia is a Brazilian conglomerate that centers around its initial constituent Banco Garantia. It added a brewery to its operations with the largest market share in Brazil and Argentina, becoming literally a monopoly in many other Latin American countries. With acquisitions in Belgium and the US, it became probably the world's leading producer of beer. The group also operates a retail chain that became the leading non-food retailer in the country and an investment company with billion-dollar investments in its portfolio. The drive behind diversification for the company and Brazil in general was the lack of efficient stock markets in the region and as insurance in response to the economic volatility in Brazil and the world in general.

This diversification was sought in the form of no consolidated corporate ownership of the affiliate businesses to minimize interdependencies and allow for flexible assembling and disassembling of groups according to the economic conditions. That of course didn't mean that the group members wouldn't share resources, operations, knowledge and expertise to reduce costs and increase revenues. Additionally the group could easily shift and engage resources to take advantage of market opportunities, either in the form of organic growth or acquisitions. Performing such tasks in a non-opportunistic way requires special skills and a great deal of understanding between the partner owners of the group. This was something that Grupo Garantia managed especially well given the continuous good market performance of the group.

The group is under the leadership of Jorge Paulo Lemann (a Harvard graduate and tennis champion) and his two partners, Carlos Sicupira, and Marcel Telles. They initially created the bank in the 1970s as the first entity of the group and later on added the remaining three business entities. While each one of them was a single legal entity, they acted and were perceived as a cohesive organization by investors, regulators and customers. The group kept the same values and operating principles enabling reputation and talent to flow across all units. As a whole the group was headed under the leadership of the three partners by a holding board mainly by investors of the group that were not involved in its management actively. Adding to that the secretive nature of its internals, the group made it difficult for somebody outside of it to make sense of who the real power centers and controllers were. It was more of a system of voting power based on performance and contribution formalized through agreements between partners than an actual account of capital holding.

Reflecting the management philosophy of its owners, each company insisted on a form of collaborative government without a rigid hierarchy that allowed talented and efficient employees to rise up to the senior levels. This approach was in contrast to the traditional favoritism observed in many large South American corporations. This was also reflected in the office arrangement in the buildings, as there was no discrimination based on level—they were all on the same floor. As a result of such practices, internal competition between employees was fierce and encouraged to ensure only the best were at the top. In support of that, salaries across the group were kept minimal and real differences were reflected in the bonuses due to performance contributions and the profits of each unit that would amount to multiples of the managers' salaries.

The conglomerate, although diversified, didn't further pursue diversification as the owners soon realized that spreading thin across more sectors would reduce the focus and attention their four units required. The group shows a remarkable sense of self-awareness that usually is not seen in similar cases and it's one that has served the conglomerate well. Apparently, and according to Grupo Garantia, there is a limit in horizontal growth past which one should focus on organic and vertical growth.

HINDUJA GROUP

The Hinduja Group is a global family conglomerate originating from India but headquartered in London. Funded before World War I, the group ventured first in Iran and then spread to the rest of the world. Its portfolio ranges from automotive, oil and gas, banking and finance, power, media, real estate, healthcare and trading among others. While the focus and majority of business activity served the Indian subcontinent and the Middle East, the company is quite active in other parts of the world. The strong family ties of the family members (with the third and fourth generation moving into management) is a key success factor for the organization. This, coupled with a distribution of responsibilities into various sectors, allows the company to venture into new territories and build its diverse portfolio.

The automotive sector of the company is the largest manufacturer of commercial vehicles in India and with factories in Czech Republic it also serves European customers with its line of trucks. In addition the group has a 50% stake with the US manufacturer John Deere in construction equipment manufacturing, a 75% stake in a leading bus maker in the United Kingdom and formed an alliance with Nissan to further enhance its automotive industry presence.

The finance sector of the company includes banking activities in Switzerland with subsidiaries in major finance hubs, and outlets and separate banking services all over India. The power sector of the conglomerate is involved in both traditional and renewable power generation with coal-fired and wind power plants in India. The real estate arm of the company is involved in major development plants in India and construction projects in areas such as oil and gas, clean energy, airports, ports, highways and waste management. The company is also active in trading metal and fertilizers and recently ventured into healthcare with a state-of-the-art hospital in Mumbai and future plans for expansion in the field.

An interesting diversification (usually seen in family business in Europe) came with the venture into the media field. The company is one of India's largest integrated media companies and one of the largest multisystem operators and providers in India. It also became a content provider with film and television productions and continues to grow in the area.

The investment philosophy of Hinduja includes the maintenance of a significant presence in multiple businesses and geographies through stock and industrial investments. Its investment philosophy encompasses short-term minority holdings as well as long-term strategic positions in constituent companies. The group keeps an open mind to potential business opportunities and wants to be viewed as catalysts that accelerate business development and growth while occasionally acting as "alchemists" in discovering new and emerging opportunities.

LONRHO

Founded in London at the beginning of the 20th century, Lonrho was initially focused on mining and agriculture in what was known as Rhodesia (now Zimbabwe). The company went through many ups and downs, from being the largest company in the country in the 1940s to losing many assets and almost liquidating in the first years of the 1960s. A decision of the key shareholders to revitalize the company under the leadership of Tiny Rowland did the job and turned the company around to prosperous times. Those were the years the company was seeking any deal it could to make money. The resulting acquisitions across Africa increased its diversified portfolio that, in addition to mining and agriculture, now included manufacturing, agribusiness, newspapers, hotels and general trade. The latter category proved to be at the time very profitable, focusing mainly on import and distribution of automobiles and farm and construction equipment.

The management philosophy at the time was more in making deals than managing the companies it was acquiring. The latter was assigned to managers who were hired for that particular purpose. Activities were organized into groups according to country or relevance to business sectors under a top manager in the role of a CEO. Given the complexity and extreme diversification of the conglomerate, each group was allowed to operate free from headquarter control and only the finances were controlled through the London-based headquarters. Regular monthly financial reports would be submitted from each group and, based on the problems that would surface, headquarters would investigate and intervene if necessary.

The company employed a monarchical structure under Rowland's leadership and was quite comfortable paying for access and influence. It was a very successful approach, ensuring the cooperation of many African leaders and bureaucrats, which led to unparalleled success for the conglomerate. These approaches, although profitable, were not the best for the image of the corporation. Additionally, and because of the luxurious lifestyle of its leader and management team, the company had a permanent cash flow problem. The frequent high dividend the company was giving to shareholders, along with difficulties in repatriating profits from Africa, also aggravated the cash flow issues it was facing.

To address the raised cash-flow issue, the company began selling its assets and reducing its dividends. A change of leadership in the 1990s followed with a modernization of corporate governance. Further change of leadership led to streamlining of the headquarters structure and a reduction of less than a third of its original size. At that time the company's portfolio included mining, hotels, sugar and general trade. To address the continuing need for cash flow, the company—in addition to selling assets—moved towards demerging some of its units and also changing its name to Lonmin. Eventually the company divested most of its non-mining assets, becoming in this way a mining company, with gold, coal and platinum assets. Regaining the respect that the company once had was another challenge that took longer to tackle.

Although Lonrho is not functioning as a multipreneur anymore, it was included here in an attempt to point out some of the issues that conglomerates face and the difficulties of horizontal diversification that we discuss in this book. There are limits to how far one organization can go under a given structure and corporate philosophy and crossing those limits can deprive organizations the ability to multipreneur.

SAMSUNG

Samsung is a Korean family conglomerate with diverse businesses that today span advanced technology, semiconductors, skyscraper and plant construction, petrochemicals, fashion, medicine, finance, hotels and more. Korean firms have in general strong Confucian beliefs that inspire order and respect for hierarchy. These are usually reflected in stiff corporate structures in contrast to the Western style of lean, autonomous and flexible units. Samsung was no exception to the rule, but the company made intentional efforts to change its culture and nowadays can compete globally as an equal player among the world's multinationals.

The magnitude of the bureaucracy was so intense that it could take up to a 21-step process for ordering simple equipment. Samsung's culture was that of imitation and the group secretariat that was controlling the conglomerate was famous for experimenting with every new and untried business field that would come to their attention without any regard of the market needs and structure.

Enforcing Western business practices in the beginning of the 1990s (dubbed the Second Foundation) led the company to apply radical reforms to make its units more flexible and responsive. A major problem for Samsung was that it focused on quantity instead of quality, as did most Korean businesses of the time. Quantity allowed lower prices and made the companies competitive in the short run. As a strategy this is successful as long as wages somewhere else in the world are not lower than your own. The leadership of Samsung realized that a switch to quality was necessary if the company was to reach its goal and become one of the leading companies in the world.

A culture that promoted quality and demoted tolerance and indifference to unacceptable defect rates was established through a variety of measures, from freezing factory lines when defects were spotted to sending employees abroad for a few years to be exposed to Western practices, to educating all middle and upper managers on globalization issues (such as subscribing them all to *Newsweek* magazine) and automating routine decision processes. The latter was also an attempt to bypass the unwieldy and top-heavy management with the highly authoritarian management style that stifled innovation and creativity. The philosophy that quantity will come with quality paid off and Samsung established itself as the number one company in Korea and one of the leading manufacturers in the world.

As the reforms were moving on in the 1990s, the company pushed even more to modernize its structure, moving a lot of the decision-making downwards to lower-level managers. Additional reform came in the form of improving the quality of life of employees by streamlining working standards to those of the industrial Western countries and allowing employees to explore social and personal activities that would enrich their lives and help them become more efficient at work. Instead of having them at work for almost 12 hours—which sometimes ended up being counterproductive as they would eventually just drift around—the company enforced an eight- to nine-hour schedule that allowed them to explore social and personal interests. Management were also required to spend most of their time moving around the plants and meeting with suppliers and customers instead of staying in their offices, as was traditionally the case. Additionally, the company began to hire women with career specialties, something that was unthinkable for Korean companies at the time. This trend increased as the traditional role of Korean women shifted from family to career.

With 370,000 employees and net sales of almost 250 billion dollars in 2012, Samsung stands as a global player in the economic arena. The core values of the company surprisingly do not include innovation, despite the fact that this giant is heavily involved and leads innovation. People and co-prosperity are listed along with integrity to emphasize the traditional collectivist values of Confucianism, despite the functional modernization of the company. Releasing the full potential of its people and the communities they serve is equally important for a company that wants to blend with society rather than distinguish itself from it.

Empowering change is another value that enables the company to anticipate market needs and demands so it can plan strategies to ensure its long-term success. This is coupled with the company's mission to excellence and commitment to develop quality products and services for the various market needs. In short, Samsung, like most other companies, wants to lead the world market but values the acceptance it receives from all parts of the society.

SIEMENS

Siemens is a German conglomerate and one of the leading corporations in the world with activities that span multiple sectors, has an employee base of 360,000 employees across 190 countries and revenue of 78.3 billion euros. It's important to see the spectrum of activities that Siemens is involved in as it serves as an ideal example of a multipreneurial corporation. From building trains, to full-scale logistics solutions, to wind turbines and smart grid solutions, to lighting products and industrial software, to CT scanners and a multitude of other medical devices and solutions, and finally real estate and financial services, Siemens has shown it can successfully innovate and spread itself into multiple industry sectors.

Like most international organizations, Siemens has distributed operations in many locations around the world. The purpose of such distribution of entities is meant to allow the company to maintain a global presence and respond to market needs as soon as they appear. Enabling the flow of knowledge between diverse organizational units is an absolute requirement for the diffusion of innovation and feedback loops amongst practitioners in Siemens. Keeping in touch is of primary importance and networking amongst employees according to their specific business topics is a practice that is encouraged and promoted throughout the organization. The term that most closely relates to what Siemens is doing is "communities of practice" (CoPs) and is based on the idea of bringing together (physically and virtually) people with the same business interests. These groups can be as small as a handful of members or as big as a couple of hundred of them and can include people from any Siemens unit from around the world. These "focus groups" allow Siemens to literally multipreneur internally by exploring in parallel opportunities in almost every aspect of the organization, from new product development, to process streamlining, to research and design.

Although CoPs are a great way to knowledge discovery and diffusion, they have some drawbacks that need to be mentioned here:

- They are ideal for established organizations with a long enough lifecycle to enable the organization to reap the benefits of the collective knowledge and innovation of its members. Smaller corporations—and especially technology and Internet start-ups—have nowadays a very small lifecycle between their creation and failure or acquisition by bigger ones with different organizational cultures than the original start-up.

- Actively involving employees in CoPs requires an investment in time and effort that will consume resources with uncertain return.

- Their value increases in time as more knowledge is exchanged and new members with fresh ideas are added.

Siemens identified certain factors as preconditions for viable CoPs that add value to the individual and the organization as a whole, including:

- *Organizing and facilitating community activities:* This is under the responsibility of management and the gatekeepers of the resources that need to be committed and handle the logistics of these operations. A moderator is usually assigned that coordinates the community activities, although spontaneous activities and interests can be self-organized.

- *Actively connect providers and consumers of knowledge:* It should be evident in the CoPs how one can reach out and find the right person to communicate to get the issue that concerns them resolved.

- *Redefining focus when needed:* CoPs are allowed to evolve as needed and redefine their purpose and scope according to their members' preferences for specific knowledge areas. Again this can be under the control of the moderator or self-organized.

- *Interacting with the community environment:* A vital function of CoPs is to inform management and other constituents of the organization's internal community of their discoveries and findings. This is a way of transforming discussions to actions that realizes the full potential of the knowledge community. Interacting with the internal community is also a way of asking for support contributions when the issue discussed requires it. It also serves as a way to advertise the CoP and recruit new members.

- *Living the community values:* Like any type of community there need to be values that keep the members together and active. Given that innovation and creativity is the purpose of most CoPs, the most essential values for viability are probably trust and openness. Members need to feel comfortable asking questions or sharing knowledge and this exchange needs to involve all the members at one time or another. In simple terms there should be a give and take (cost-benefit) that all members contribute and they all benefit from the community.

Siemens is a company with a strong emphasis on innovation that chose to grow mainly organically. Innovation is one of the three core values (the other two being responsible and excellence) of the company that shaped its vision and formed the strategy of the company to achieve sustainable and profitable growth. To achieve its primary goal to be the "pioneer", almost 10% of its workforce is involved in new products and solutions for the sectors it supports.

SWIRE GROUP

With roots in England towards the beginning of the 19th century, the Swire Group is probably the oldest conglomerate in existence. Starting as a family business and moving around to almost every continent in the world, the group's major operations were finally hosted in Hong Kong. Initial activities included shipping, sugar refineries and paint manufacturing. As a result of World War II, the company lost most of its assets and was forced to start again from the beginning.

Within a few years after the end of the war the company managed to rebuild its key operational businesses of sugar refining, dockyard and paint manufacturing. Looking to explore new opportunities, the company developed an aircraft maintenance facility capitalizing on the engineering skill of its dockyard group. Further development came in the form of mergers and acquisitions with rival companies that eventually built into one of the world's leaders in its field. This was followed by the acquisition of Cathay Pacific Airways, which soon became one of the most successful airlines in the region.

In the 1950s the company expanded its shipping services and re-established headquarters in Australia and invested in the road and cold storage sectors, eventually becoming the biggest refrigerated truck operator in Australia. In the 1960s the company acquired a bottling business in Hong Kong and became one of the biggest bottlers for Coca-Cola. In the next decade the company ventured into properties and enhanced its portfolio with prestigious properties developed and managed by the group.

In the 1980s the group began to reinvest in mainland China, expanding its Coca-Cola production business and trading interests along with aircraft engineering and paint manufacturing. Following that expansion in the 2000s, the company acquired the world's largest tea trading operations with substantial agricultural interests in Africa and Sri Lanka. Additionally, the group acquired Australia's largest construction and demolition waste recycler, increased its investments in mainland China and ventured into the hotel business.

The group now employs over 120,000 people worldwide, has its headquarters in London and still retains the "family" flavor as a number of members of the Swire family are actively involved in the business. The company's motto is action-oriented with operational excellence as one of its core values. Growing the talents of its staff and investing in their commitment is another value that allows the company to enjoy sustainable growth even in hard economic times.

TOSHIBA

Toshiba Corporation is a Japanese conglomerate with a diverse portfolio of products and services ranging from personal computers, electronics, telecommunication, semiconductors, home appliances, medical equipment, elevators, escalators, office equipment and lighting to logistics and IT services. Toshiba is a conglomerate that can build almost anything, from a laptop to a nuclear reactor.

The company is a classic case of a company that sought diversification to achieve sustainable growth. Investing and operating diverse market sectors allows the company to handle market volatility and sustain industries where growth is low with earnings from high-growth sectors until the market recovers. An example of such balancing was the 1998 consolidate sales where the steep drop of semiconductor and power station business was compensated by the earnings from its computer sector.

Japan's industrial growth has been grounded on a strong factory-based competitiveness and Toshiba is a classic example of it. One of the secrets of its continuing success is the establishment of high-tech manufacturing sites that integrate its human capital and resources to produce knowledge-intensive corporate communities. These knowledge-intensive sites are focused and versatile and allow the company to enhance its capabilities as a manufacturer and innovator.

Toshiba's philosophy that innovation can happen everywhere, from the factory floor to the executive boardroom, is one of its secrets for staying competitive. It's a diffuse quality that empowers everyone to feel creative and important about what they are doing. To achieve that it created a cross-divisional structure to enable economies of scope in the sharing of tacit and explicit knowledge. By adopting an enabling context, knowledge can be shared and ideas can be filtered at the corporate level, allowing contributions and feedback from diverse decisions. It is the sharing at the higher levels where basic values and the culture of knowledge creation are enforced and spread throughout the organization. This is a vital strategy for Toshiba and is seen as a required adaptation to the volatile economic environment of our times.

To address the need for cross-divisional communication Toshiba created as early as 1984 the Advanced-I Group ("I" stands for "information", "integration" and "intelligence"). It was built for speed and had the autonomy to act quickly to address the developing market of portable computers initially and later on in guiding Toshiba into the multimedia age. The taskforce was assembled from different divisions, such as information systems, power systems and industrial equipment, leading to a cross-discipline team that was able to leverage the different expertise and come up with innovative solutions such as notebook computers, mobile personal digital assistants, DVD players and smart TVs, to name a few.

Handing such initiatives to the divisions would defeat their purpose, as divisions wouldn't risk jeopardizing their performance with potential failures and would usually suppress any risky initiative at the sign of mounting difficulties. Risk-taking and tolerance to failure was a vital ingredient if the team was going to succeed in creating new products and venture into new markets, so establishing such a philosophy was a vital ingredient of the initiative. To enforce such spirit, Toshiba realized that top executive support was essential, so it made sure the management committee included a senior executive vice president and three directors appointed as deputy executives. To reflect the diversity required for such a team, the chief technology executives of all of Toshiba's divisions became regular members of these committees. During the meetings the members would share business ideas and updates and decide on what is worth following up and explore new product possibilities. Having the major decision-makers together also made it easy to set up ad hoc teams by nominating and involving the right people from their divisions and departments. In that sense the division heads would serve as knowledge bases of the expertise in their sectors, in addition to personally endorsing the initiatives. Having a personal stake ensured the commitment of resources and personnel that made project realizations a success.

The idea behind these initiatives was to dissipate knowledge across organizational silos, enabling technologies and human expertise to benefit from the interaction and innovate for new products and services. Through such initiatives, Toshiba has managed to venture into new territories and become a truly multipreneurial corporation. Spreading the knowledge gains globally was another way for the company to expand its knowledge base and benefit from contributions from its global workforce. In addition, the global spread allowed the company to tap (especially in R&D) into the brains and creativity of different cultures with different educational systems and different beliefs, enabling in this way the company to gain an understanding of the global market.

5.3   The Government Case

Based on the organizational adoption of multipreneurship that we have seen so far, it should be apparent that the government ideally qualifies for multipreneurial activities. Government's traditional role in the economy has been to create the conditions for growth, control fair play and intervene when "market fixing" is required. Government's entrepreneurial ventures are usually expected as social endeavors where the return on the investment would be low for private investors to consider. Tending to minorities of the population, providing healthcare services, ensuring law and order and funding cultural and basic research initiatives are some of the types of role that governments traditionally expect to assume.

History can also serve as guide. For the ancient Athenians and the other Greek city states, for example, it was the government-led initiatives to colonize new territories that spread their reach and enabled commerce and entrepreneurship to flourish. The return on those investments is evident in the wealth of knowledge and wisdom the West inherited through art, philosophy, science and engineering. Waging war to acquire access to resources (although not suggested now), it was a pure state decision that was followed by privateers and entrepreneurs who exploited the opportunities that new territories provided. Wars are not necessary anymore today because resources can be accessed through trade and unilateral agreements.

Unfortunately, due mainly to worldwide economic instability, governments nowadays have become conservative in their ventures to the point of being considered an obstacle in the dynamic world we live in. Its sluggishness due to size and weight makes its existence necessary but counterproductive. While their attempts to cut back to foster recovery from crisis can be justified as first responses, governments also claim that letting the private sector lead is meant to unleash the potential of entrepreneurs that will create businesses and stimulate growth. This contrast, while convenient for politicians, is nevertheless counterproductive and misleading since, as we believe, the role of the state is vital as an enabler of growth.

In the name of efficiency governments move more and more towards outsourcing to the private sector more and more of their functions. Most of the time, though, this outsourcing is inefficient as the costs of monitoring and controlling the quality of the service it provides does not result in lowering the costs or the quality of the services it substitutes. A case in point is the outsourcing of the London 2012 Olympics security to a private firm that couldn't eventually deliver, leading to the state intervening and taking up the cost of the service.

The important question nowadays is whether the government should become more forthcoming in adopting the entrepreneurial attitudes of private businesses and become a risk-taker, even leading initiatives and reaping higher rewards for its citizens. Instead of that, we witness nowadays the government moving away from dynamic, competitive and innovative initiatives that involve risk and moving towards debt reduction by privatizing and outsourcing a lot of its functions.

What is not evident nowadays, primarily because of the passive role governments take in leading change, is that in the past some if not all the major accomplishments in science, technology and the economy have been government initiatives. Revolutionary innovations such as the Internet, GPS, space exploration, nanotechnology and medical breakthroughs, to name a few, were all made possible due to government initiatives and funding. All of these discoveries and innovations spilled over into the corporate world that created businesses that capitalized on them.

Some of the most visible cases of government impact on innovation include:

- The National Science Foundation (NSF) of the US funded the development of the algorithm that led to Google's success.

- The UK Medical Research Council (MRC) funded discoveries that established the foundations for modern biotechnology.

- The US Small Business Innovation Research (SBIR) public venture capital was used to fund some of the most innovative young companies, most notably Apple. The case of Apple is also interesting as some of its high-profile products, such as the iPhone, are based on technologies funded by the US government.

- The US Defense Advanced Research Projects Agency enabled and commercialized the Internet.

- BNDES is Brazil's state investment bank, which takes risks financing biotech and cleantech sectors that venture capitalists and private banks avoid. The bank enjoyed great returns on its investments in such sectors, paving the way for private organizations to join and take over. The earnings from such activities can more than compensate the losses and leave plenty for the government to invest in sectors such as education and healthcare.

- The National Aeronautics and Space Administration in the US is probably the sole enabler of space technology breakthroughs in the Western world.

- The Chinese Development Bank led many successful initiatives in high-risk green economic initiatives

The market by itself would have either taken much more time or never managed to invest in and realize these innovations by itself. These developments forced economists to consider innovation and technology as major drivers of economic growth instead of as an external parameter of economic models. A case where the government might lead entrepreneurship nowadays is in launching clean technologies, such as wind turbines and solar panels, which would provide the initial push for the establishment of these technologies. This effort can also indirectly lead to funding entrepreneurs in the field. The gains are multiple as they include better living conditions for citizens as well as motivation and support for private initiatives and the establishment of new industries.

The modern expectations of governments are not to engage and invest in things the private sector is already doing, even if they can be done better, but to invest and exploit areas/opportunities out of the reach of private sectors. Strong vision, will and commitment are necessary, but in addition sector- and technology-specific expertise is required. This means recruiting appropriate talent, under inspired leadership, and establishing the processes that will make things happen. The government nowadays is not just expected to be a market controller balancing private and social returns, but to also be a leader in R&D producing and diffusing knowledge throughout the economy.

All of these examples mentioned above are cases where the state took an active role in multipreneuring and leading innovation and change, reducing the risk in new territories and making them attractive for private actors to enter. Although today in many cases, due to the volatility of the economic environment, the state might be reluctant to engage wholeheartedly in high-risk ventures, one does expect it to be a key partner of the private sector—and at times the brave one that takes most of the risk. Accommodating interest groups that don't align with this philosophy should be drastically reduced and the direction of government should focus on advancing the well-being of all of its citizens. Even in the worst case when governments need to return the support they received, they can at least require some alignment from their partners on risk-taking initiatives.

Governments should never allow themselves to be viewed as inefficient versions of the private sector, as this will make it the least desirable partner in public–private collaborations and disadvantage it spearheading innovations that could in return limit the rewards it deserves. This is vital as it will allow the government to be independent from pressures and demands from private interests. In addition, public investments should not be seen as business giveaways for a select few to explore and become rich; they should always be tied to some kind of return for the public good.

Chapter 6
Multipreneurship Framework

A theory of entrepreneurship that will also include multipreneurship should emerge naturally from an economic theory, in the same sense that tornados and hurricanes should naturally emerge from any theory that describes the weather. Although early contributions to understanding multipreneurship have been noted in the literature, a comprehensive description of the phenomenon still eludes theoretical framing.

Dealing with its complexities requires a multidisciplinary attack from diverse fields such as:

- economics, for the expression of its monetary and financial aspects

- psychology, for the cognitive and emotional states of those involved

- sociology, for the influences and implications of the human environment

- mathematics, for network representation and understanding

- physics, to express its dynamic nature (forces, pressures and rates of change) and its emergent character (complexity).

This type of intervention is also a reflection of some of the inadequacies of the theoretical framings of entrepreneurship that don't seem to stand the test of time. Having said that, this chapter attempts to contribute to the understanding of the phenomenon of multipreneurship by following a multidisciplinary perspective, primarily because of its human, social and economic dimensions, which all contribute to its appearance. In this way their contribution are vital in explaining its multifaceted attributes and provide some foundation for its theoretical framing.

A clarification here is necessary to dissolve any illusion of a full, detailed and scientifically rigorous theoretical framework. Social science deals by default with social issues and as such it is affected by the diversity of human reasoning, motivation and perspectives. In that sense every individual and organization is unique and "cloning" them based on a theory is in the sphere of science fiction (at least for now). Having a theory that explains every detail of all these unique individuals and organizations will defeat the purpose of a theory (not to mention we will run out of paper), which is to simplify and abstract reality in a model, so it can be easily useable and efficient in making predictions.

The ideal theory of multipreneurship should be a simplification of reality that enlightens and advises practitioners and policy-makers. Our attempt here will follow this practice and try to provide a framework for multipreneurship that will explain behavior and the workings of the phenomenon in its majority and not for every possible case that could exist out there. Also, we hope that the developed framework will trigger discussion that will extend and expand the understanding of multipreneurship in a constructive way.

In building the theory (and more or less any theory), we need to include and define:

- the set of elements (mathematical variables in a strict sense) that abstract the objects and concepts needed for its explanation

- the well-defined relationships (mathematical functions in a strict sense) that connect/relate its elements

- provide explanations for the rationale behind the form of the relationships we established

- express everything as a model in a formal way, such as in a formula or graphic using elementary representative forms and shapes.

Looking into the past (Penrose 1955), the fundamental research question upon which theories of entrepreneurship were developed was how to account for the existence and successful growth of the firm as reflected in the vision of its owner and entrepreneur.

Obviously firms don't grow out of nothing and regardless of how small the beginnings, one still needs some wood and a spark to light a fire, even in a location that is windy and rainy. On top of that (following the previous analogy), there has to be a way to make one fire more attractive than another if more people/customers are to be attracted to it. The vision of the entrepreneur naturally seems to be a key ingredient for the creation and success of his firm, but it is not enough by itself to make things happen.

We will approach entrepreneurship and by extension multipreneurship by looking at all the possible ways to start our questioning following the interrogatives "diamond" (probe diamond) of Figure 6.1. This process might lead to more answers than questions but hopefully the spread of the inquiry will eventually converge to a solid enough description of the phenomenon to allow for useful conclusions to be drawn. The horizontal plane of the "When", "Where", "Who" and "What" form represents the perceived reality upon which interpretations ("How") will be made and perceptions ("Why") formed.

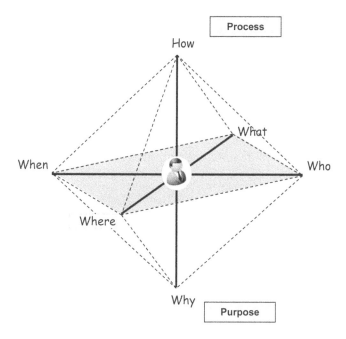

Figure 6.1   The interrogatives diamond in scientific research

In our analysis we will assume that the differences between perception and reality (Figure 6.2) are not dramatic enough to distort cognition in individuals (at least the successful ones) and affect entrepreneurial decision-making. A perfect match in any way is impossible as the act of retrospection and interpretation of reality takes effort and time, so in essence a rational actor can

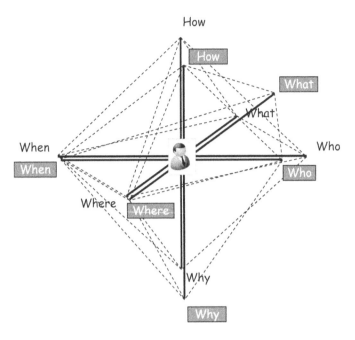

**Figure 6.2   Differences between perception and reality along
four dimensions**

only account for past realities. Also the norm of human activities is considered here and not special cases, which would include deviations in the explanation in the form of outliers.

This line of inquiry can repeat itself until satisfactory explanations are reached and sense-making is ready to form strategies to counter environmental triggers such as entrepreneurial opportunities and the plans entrepreneurs form to exploit them. The aspects each vertex addresses in our case include:

- "When": the time interval from the search for an opportunity to its full exploitation. This is similar to the time dimension of physical phenomena and in our case it will be a path the entrepreneur followed in time.

- "Where": the geographical and virtual places where all action took place.

- "Who": represents the entities involved, including the entrepreneur, his partners, the institutions and organizations involved in the process of the venture formation and operation and, of course, intermediaries and customers.

- "What": this includes descriptions of actions, processes and activities surrounding the discovery and exploitation of entrepreneurial opportunity.

- "How": the decision-making process.

- "Why": the motivations and rationale behind intentions and actions that led to decisions.

It must be apparent from the multiple cases presented in the previous chapters that at the beginning, when they build their ventures, multipreneurs focus more on "How" than anything else. Most other people will spend too much time on "What" and try to understand and make sense of the "Why", while multipreneurs will breeze through these states and get involved in how they will make things happen. Ordinary people might feel limited in terms of internal strength and motivation in following through with the endeavor or feel comfortable having accomplished this in their mind. Entrepreneurs, on the other hand, have a tremendous need to materialize that motivates them to see this happening in front of them.

Another way would be to see entrepreneurship from the point of view of setting a goal and accomplishing it. Setting a goal can be psychologically self-defeating if one is excessively focusing on the outcome instead of the process. Keeping the end result vivid in mind can be quite satisfying and mentally exhaustive and can suppress critical and creative thinking, eventually draining one from the will to move further. To counter this hypnotic effect of visualizing the end result, one needs to engage their reserves of willpower and attention control. The way that some entrepreneurs make their ideas realistic is by putting things in writing, either by jotting shapes with words and numbers that represent the concept of a venture or in more formal ways in the form of proposals and business plans.

For the case of multipreneurship, the theoretical literature is limited in addressing the question of how and when multipreneurial behavior is likely to be observed. Answering these questions will also address the questions of why and when we are likely to observe the formation of diverse business groups under the same ownership and control. A theory will need to differentiate and explain why in some cases mature entrepreneurs choose to invest in expanding their existing business activities and in others they move towards diversification and venture into new industries. The latter case incurs great administrative and knowledge costs that require a different skill set than the ones involved in organic growth and expansion into an already familiar industry.

To summarize the theoretical needs of our endeavor, a theory of multipreneurship, in addition to complying with the explanation of entrepreneurship in the first place, will have to explain the following:

- Why do some individuals who are already entrepreneurs gravitate towards exploring and building diverse ventures?

- How is multipreneurship evolved from entrepreneurship?

- At what time does it express itself?

- What are the inherent and acquired qualities that support the expression of multipreneurship?

- Under what conditions do multipreneurial attributes flourish?

With these needs in mind we will try to highlight the elements that seem to characterize multipreneurial attitude and the conditions that allow them to flourish. The analysis that follows will break the phenomenon into distinct parts that include the individual with his personal attributes and social circles and the market that facilitates the expression of entrepreneurship and, by extension, of multipreneurship. After this, we will present the process of discovering and exploiting opportunities and hopefully bring everything together into a cohesive and descriptive framework.

6.1   The Individual Entrepreneur

Entrepreneurs—as is widely accepted—are people who function under risk and manage to create and operate one or many businesses. As such they can be viewed as knowledge systems that are shaped and mature personally and professionally under the influence of different genetic and environmental factors. Such factors are responsible for the transformation of information to knowledge and the formation of the entrepreneurs' perceptions of the world around them. They also directly influence the identification of opportunities and structure the decision-making process for their exploitation. For the purposes of our analysis here we will consider a systems perspective of four

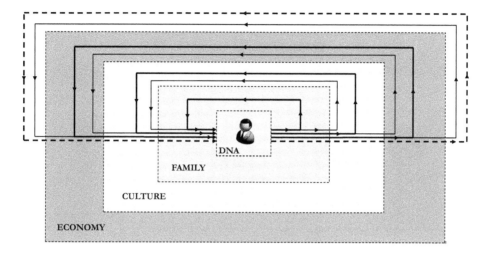

Figure 6.3   Systems representation of the environmental influences on an individual

generalized layers, each one influencing the way messages travel to and from the entrepreneur (Figure 6.3).

Starting with the inherited genetic traits that are passed to each one of us through DNA from our ancestors and moving on to the family and social environments, we grow and learn to operate in families (or their substitutes) that exist in societies. As microcosms inside nations, regions and the world at large, these groups influence individuals at different times and stages in their development and leave marks that in some people trigger and nurture the expression of selective attributes that lead to entrepreneurship. More specifically the layers shown encase: (1) inherited personality and intelligence (DNA imprinting); (2) family environments where we grew up and matured and that conditioned us to certain beliefs and values; (3) the society we live in that imposes cultural traits in us; and (4) the economy at large with its global trends and influences. Some of the influences that penetrate and guide our perspective and purpose in the world are education and personal experiences. These influence personal style and build intellectual abilities and coping skills throughout our lifetime.

Because the exposure to each of these layers takes place at different times in the life of an entrepreneur, we should be able to identify their influence trace on the attributes and characteristics of the individual. As Figure 6.4, shows each environmental layer encloses and exerts primary influence on the ones

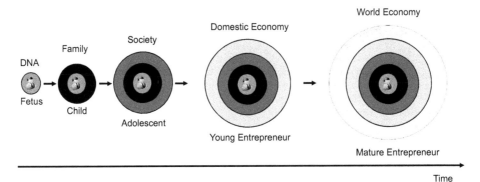

Figure 6.4   Influence circles in the evolution of entrepreneurs

it encloses and to a lesser degree its outside layers through feedback from the inside ones. In other words, as we are influenced by the world, we also influence the world, at least in our vicinity. Major modes of interaction include family values, education, and the political and economic environments of the society in which one grows up. This "onion" of rings influences our perceptions of other people and the situations we are in and impacts our decision-making process and the way we behave and act. Similar influences are exerted on other

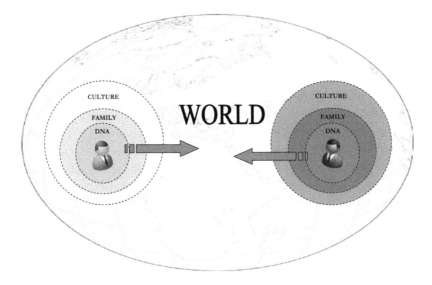

Figure 6.5   Influence circles in communication process

people, resulting in a communication process that is filtering messages as they travel from one person to another (Figure 6.5).

To a person these influences are affected by education and experience while interacting with others. Each one of us moves in the world surrounded by these "onion" rings of influence, filtering incoming signals that people and events emit, and modulating the signals we emit. Personality and culture are the primary expressions of this filtering that we do. Multipreneurs need to be aware of this layering if they are to communicate the right message to the right recipient across cultures and make sense of what they receive in return.

What saves us from the confusion of communicating through these layers is the simple fact that we are all more or less the same in terms of genetic characteristics; our societies generally look alike in terms of familial and social structures and we all share the same world. It is a certainty that we have a lot (if not most) things in common, so these commonalities would form the foundation upon which we base our communication with others and enhance our ability to cooperate and grow together.

The abstraction of layers of influence allows us to depict differences between people in terms of the extent of the influence of each layer. For someone such as an orphan, for example, (Figure 6.6) who didn't grow in a family environment, the influence of a close family environment is expected to be less, so the impact of his surrounding culture is bound to make a stronger impression than in other individuals. The replacement of family values with cultural ones could result in emotional gaps and unfulfilled needs, such as the feeling of safety that families usually provide. Similarly, if the society one lives in is isolationist (such as Albania in the 1970s), the world economy and trends will have very little impact and influence and culture will play the role that an extended economy would normally play. People from such environments are not going to feel comfortable venturing outside the border of their societies as to them that is uncharted territory.

Another important element of our representation is that the borders between layers are flexible and at times could extend into each other, as the concepts/entities they represent can have overlapping properties and the influences on one another vary from one individual to another. Overall the distinct regions of influence of Figures 6.3, 6.6 and 6.7 are deemed adequate for the needs of a theoretical framework that addresses entrepreneurship and, by extension, multipreneurship.

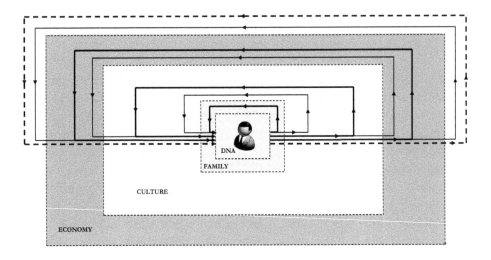

Figure 6.6   Individual with small family influence

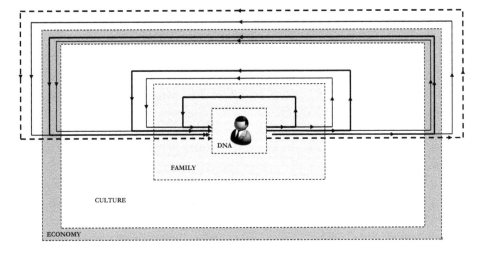

Figure 6.7   Individual isolated from the global economy

INHERITED AND DEVELOPMENTAL TRAITS

There is the undeniable truth that we all come to life with certain physical features that affect the way we perceive the world and others. Some people can be naturally talented towards speaking many languages, while others can perform fast arithmetic calculations, to name a few of these traits. This also extends to the emotional world, where some people show mild temperament, while others tend to lose patience more easily and become aggressive in conflicts.

In the same way that it is unlikely for someone to be a professional basketball player with a height of 1 meter, it is unlikely to see multipreneurs with low IQ or cognitive disabilities. While intelligence is genetic, entrepreneurs could benefit a lot from self-awareness that could highlight their strengths and weaknesses. Being aware of their personal traits and coming to terms with them is vital for understanding the environment, strategizing about new ventures and selecting the best approach to achieve their goals.

Another set of influences comes from the family environment in which we are raised and mature as individuals. This environment provides our first exposure to other human beings and as a result influences our character and personality and forms the core of our values and norms. It serves as the mirror that displays our reflection on others and, according to the way we are perceived, we form our personality, our principles and values about ourselves and others. As children and teenagers we are powerless most of the time to control any of these influences or modify our memories of past experiences, so the most we can hope is to be aware of these influences and come to terms with them. The only difference here with our inherited traits is our ability to rationalize and intellectually adapt those family and early social values that don't serve us well, to what we believe can enhance our personalities and ensure success in our adult lives.

The innermost filters of our perception are composed of our values, beliefs, interests, needs, goals and expectations at each instant in time along with our understanding of situations and our communication capabilities. All of these, when combined with our cognitive abilities to generalize, hypothesize and deduct, form our personality and define the way we interact with our environment. Self-awareness is of primary importance in being effective in what we do and communicating business ideas, whether face-to-face or electronic, is no exception to the rule.

When faced with a problem, most people will come up with a solution or an action list, either by analysis or synthesis. In terms of logic, this is like applying deductive or inductive reasoning. Breaking a problem down into its constituent parts and studying its individual elements can help reveal the greater picture in a methodological/scientific approach, while studying cases and discovering common elements can help identify what's common and thus persistent in them. We can achieve the first by applying existing knowledge to create a new one, while the latter uses generalizations to arrive at first principles. In the case of entrepreneurship both deductive and inductive logic is necessary, as opportunities need to be broken down in their constituent parts so that each one is tackled successfully and at the same time similarities between ventures need to be leveraged if efficiencies of scale are to be achieved.

CULTURE

Culture can be defined as an expression of the common perceptions and experiences among members of a group, a community or a nation. Organizations can be included in this description as special categories of communities of interests. Through sharing common experiences, groups create their own unique interaction environment, leading to the development of unique sets of values—that is, broad tendencies to prefer a certain state of affairs over others—and practices—that is, visible manifestations to an outside observer such as symbols, heroes and rituals.

If we were to break down culture to some of its constituent elements, we could say it includes language, lifestyle, dress and behavioral code, perceptions of the status and role of gender, and social interaction styles. A general classification of cultures based on orientation includes:

- *Task-oriented (linear-active):* highly organized that prefers to do things incrementally. They like structure, follow procedures and always stick to plans since time dictates schedule for them. They prefer independence to obligation so they will only reluctantly accept presents. They rely on logic to resolve conflicts. They are punctual, value their privacy and don't express emotions. In an entrepreneurial context these attributes are important for the exploitation phase of a business opportunity.

- *People-oriented (multi-active):* prefer to establish personal relationships as a foundation for business relationships. They therefore see professional life as an extension of personal life. In this type of culture favors are seen as a means of persuasion. They are flexible to changes as time doesn't represent structure for them. They tend to be extroverted, outgoing and emotional, and tend to consider schedule as a flexible item. These characteristics in the context of entrepreneurship are essential for forming networks that could assist in both the discovery and exploitation processes of an opportunity.

- *Introverted (reactive):* they tend to act in response to others, so they are also referred to as reactive. They also prefer personal interactions as a foundation for personal relationships. They are concerned with losing face, therefore avoid confrontation. This is also extended to the loss of face they might cause to others. They tend to be introverted, very respectful of others, with a calm demeanor, along with being punctual. These characteristics are not as strong in entrepreneurs as they feel quite comfortable taking risk that could potentially expose them and impact their image.

In addition to the above, classification research also identified general characteristics of cultures that lie along different dimensions. While these are inclusive in the previous types, it is worth presenting them separately.

For the purposes of this book we will consider the following five as the more influential in the emergence of multipreneurship and entrepreneurship in general:

1. *Individualist/collectivist:* refers to the degree to which the common values and beliefs of the community emphasize the needs of the individual instead of the needs of the group. In an individualistic culture there is an emphasis on personal needs and goals, regardless of whether they negotiate for themselves or for the group. Naturally in the case of entrepreneurs individualistic characteristics are dominant, although collectivist attributes are also observed, especially in the case of multipreneurs (as we will see later) and at later stages in the life of successful entrepreneurs where legacy issues play a considerable role.

2. *Power distance:* is a measure of the perception of and attitude towards authority and power. A characteristic of high power distance cultures is a strong sense of hierarchy with set rules of communications and decision-making between different levels of the hierarchy. The case of multipreneurs is usually one of low power distance as rules usually work against improvisation and the expression of free will that is vital for entrepreneurial growth.

3. *Masculinity/femininity:* refers to the importance of masculine characteristics, such as achievement and material orientation in the culture, versus feminine characteristics, such as the quality of life of people and relationships between them. This is probably the clearest case that multipreneurship is a masculine attribute as it directly and strongly relates to achievement.

4.   *Time:* describes the degree of structure we impose on our lives in
      relation to time. In unstructured/polychronic cultures people tend
      to involve themselves in parallel activities with many more people,
      while in very structured/monochronic cultures people tend to focus
      on one activity at a time and involve only people related to this
      activity. While polychronic cultures may seem chaotic, it is actually
      that culture's outlook on life that is different. In essence, polychronic
      cultures live for the present while monochronic cultures live for the
      future. In literature, polychronic cultures are referred to as having
      non-linear perception of time, while monochronic ones have more of
      a linear perception of time. Obviously the case of multipreneurship
      is by definition in the polychronic time dimension.

5.   *Context:* is a vital aspect of sense-making as it enriches our perceptions
      of situations beyond the literal meanings that appearances and
      messages carry. In high-context cultures the context of a message is
      interpreted within the context of its transmission as shaped by its
      environment. This includes the physical environment and the social
      environment with its power relationships and roles, in addition
      to the economic and political environment where entrepreneurial
      activities takes place. High-context cultures require a variety of
      information types and sources to form impression and like building
      intimate relationships. As a result social structures and hierarchies
      are more prevalent. Respect is vital for preserving the social structure
      and etiquette dictates a lot of the interactions. On the other side, low-
      context cultures include people who are highly individualized; they
      form fewer connections with each other (looking rather alienated
      and fragmented) and in general value their individuality and
      "freedom" as a birth-given right that can be exercised at any time.
      Social structures and legal systems are formed in a way that allows
      and encourages expressions of freedom and entrepreneurship.
      Regarding multipreneurship this dimension is expressed more as a
      low-context aspect, although certain characteristics of low context,
      such as hierarchies and social structures in the form of organizations
      and networks, play an important role.

The dimensions we just mentioned, although they are meant to represent
independent and unrelated characteristics, do relate to or, more accurately,
influence each other, especially when one is considering individuals. For example,
the perception of time and, as a consequence, the perception of self in time is
related to the individualistic tendencies one might have. Based on the finite life

expectancy of human beings, the perception that time passes (and thus brings everyone closer to an end) forces people to value their individual identities more and try to exert more control over their lives. This eventually leads them to form more structured life and business practices. If, on the other hand, the passage of time is not in focus, people seem to value the present more and that leads them to value their surroundings and look more at their relationships as a frame of reference for their personal identity. Those that tend to value self more tend to also value their path in time as "unique" and distinct and spend much effort and energy in preserving that path. This makes them more closed to themselves since they don't want to expose themselves to risks that might endanger that path.

Understanding the cultural context in which emotions are displayed is important for knowing how to manage those involved in entrepreneurial activities. In terms of the entrepreneurial process, culture can be seen as practices and values that frequently show up and uniquely characterize individual behavior. These practices can influence the leadership and managerial style of entrepreneurs such as the degree of centralization of authority, formalization of communication, and depth of organizational hierarchy they will adopt in their ventures. Values refer to entrepreneurs' preferences in making task execution and coordination decisions. Both categories influence micro-level behavioral patterns in individuals. The presence or absence of culture as a decisive factor in entrepreneurship has been debated frequently and while there might not be sufficient scientific evidence to suggest a direct relationship of culture and outcome, it is a parameter that no one can ignore. Especially at the nation level it is evident that political regimes can dramatically influence entrepreneurial attitudes. For example, someone born in a strongly capitalist economy such as the US has a different predisposition towards entrepreneurship than one born in a communist or totalitarian regime that suppresses individual freedom of ownership and control of a business.

The business world revolves around certain values that to a greater or lesser extent exist in every culture and organization. These include perceptions about fair play, status, image, self-preservation, objectivity and formality, to name a few. Misunderstandings usually occur from the different weight each group and individual places on each one of them. Objectivity and merit can be really compromised in certain regions, such as China and the Arab world, where nepotism is important. Ancestry dictates positions in many cases and this impacts entrepreneurial attitudes as risk-taking may lead to negative outcomes and can be taken quite personally and impact whole chains of relationships beyond any economic impact. Cultures that value consensus, such as the Japanese, would be expected to look at entrepreneurship as a more inclusive activity with considerable social impact and as such they will consider its role and benefits for the whole society. Other cultures, such as the US, have more of an individualistic nature and the winner-gets-all attitude is quite persistent (no place for second place), so entrepreneurship is viewed more as a personal and exclusive achievement of the individual.

Real problems in entrepreneurship arise when opposing cultures meet in international settings. These problems might inhibit one from expanding worldwide and suppress otherwise successful attributes of entrepreneurs. A low-context entrepreneur might believe he made his business idea explicit in a textual message to his international partners while his high-context partner might still be waiting on the non-textual aspects of the message before forming an opinion. In such situations, successful low-context entrepreneurs seem to go the extra mile to enhance the communication with additional actions such as making a phone call to introduce themselves and engaging in social banter with the other party before addressing any issue.

As shown in Chapter 4, high-profile multipreneurs favor logic and rationality over emotions and feeling. Although this might be counterintuitive and not apparent at first, the way they approach and pursue diverse ventures is supportive of that notion. Exhibiting instinctive behavior in their choice of the opportunity they pursue will be followed by a quite methodical and realistic approach to exploiting the opportunity at the expense of emotions and feelings. New ventures always involve risk that by itself carries negative feelings and avoidance, discouraging someone from pursuing risky opportunities. Even when at the beginning excitement rules, emotions by themselves are not enough to ensure proper planning and execution of business ideas. Successful multipreneurs are quite logical and methodical in the actualization phases when they exploit opportunities. As such they express characteristics of low-context cultures.

6.2   Internal Capital

In every theory that attempts to explain human behavior, such as the one we are trying to develop here for multipreneurship, one needs some variables that can express the particular "being" (essence of substance if you want) that drives individuals who are involved in the phenomenon under study. In the same way as when we study gravity we adopt mass as the property that represents entities in gravitational fields, we need a concept that incorporates the characteristics of the individual that contribute to his interaction with the entities that comprise the phenomenon. Traditional entrepreneurship theories are based on the constructs of *human* and *social capital*. These notions, although they allow for some of the observed characteristics of entrepreneurship to be expressed, do so in a way that divides them in an overlapping and not complementary way. That is primarily because the boundaries between the two seem blurred due to various interpretations given by various researchers.

Instead of using these traditional notions we will introduce here a division of the entrepreneurial attributes and characteristics into two mutually exclusive categories—*internal* and *external* capital. This division, as we will see, facilitates the conversion of one to another that we believe is vital for explaining multipreneurship. In correspondence with human capital, in internal capital we include all the innate or acquired capabilities of the entrepreneur that are part of him during his lifetime and serve as guides in his decision-making process. These include among others any genetic traits he inherited from his parents, skills that he acquired through education and training and the knowledge he gained/accumulated during his life (professional included here). We include here the entrepreneur's intellectual and cognitive capabilities, his emotional and personality attributes along with any other competencies and skills he might have. As a variable, internal capital represents the entrepreneur's state and as such it characterizes his place in time, meaning that there is a value that internal capital has at every instant in time for every individual (Figure 6.8).

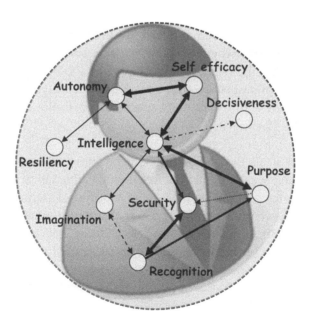

Figure 6.8   Internal capital as a network of traits

A reference to self-awareness as a contributor to internal capital needs to be mentioned here. This is important in addressing the difference between perception and reality from the point of view of an entrepreneur (illustrated in Figure 6.2). Normally there is a difference between what we perceive our traits and capabilities are and what they really are. We might think for example that we are exceptionally smart, while in reality we are average. In the entrepreneurship case we might believe we are persistent and insightful enough to succeed, while in reality these qualities are not strong enough in us to make things happen (in the business world anyway). A usual misconception that people usually make is regarding their communication skills. The plethora or disputes stand as testimony to that. By introducing self-awareness as a part of internal capital we can get away from the complication of introducing separate variables for each entrepreneurial trait to represent its real and perceived values. Self-awareness acts always as an internal filter modifier to self-efficacy and other traits required in entrepreneurship such as devotion, savviness, and networking and communication skills, to name a few.

Including entities in internal capital doesn't mean these entities are completely independent from each other. Given the range of personality and physical traits that appear in literature, one can naturally assume there will be dependencies. For example, one can be logical and mature but it's unlikely that he will be considered mature if he is illogical. In that sense there is a direct connection between the two and that is what Figure 6.8 tries to display for some hypothetical parameters of internal capital. The thickness of the connecting lines is meant to indicate the strength of the dependence between traits—the thicker the line, the stronger the relationship. If we wanted to be more sophisticated we could even adopt dashed lines for tentative relationships and colored lines to emphasize patterns of connectivity specific to particular activities such as entrepreneurship (see below).

Ideally, and if all the attributes could be measured and expressed in quantitative terms, we would be able to adopt a mathematical formalism that would express internal capital in the form of a formula. In terms of parameters we use today this formula would be a combination of what we describe as intelligence quotient, emotional quotient, knowledge, beliefs and aspirations, social networks, and physical state and resources (including monetary) under the control of the individual. Given all that, we also need to mention here that humans—being vessels of human capital—will have limitations on the amounts of each they can carry. Seen as a vessel with various compartments of fixed size, there are limits to the "quantities" of each trait (for example intelligence) as well as limits to the total of these quantities individuals can carry. This is a very important consideration as it places limits onto what one can do in accordance with the physical and mental limits of our species.

To make the distinction between human capital and the internal capital we introduced here more clearly, we will summarize the most common characteristics between the two:

- Human capital is primarily meant to address traits and qualities accrued through life experience such as coping, cognitive and management and leadership skills. Although these traits also imply there is a foundation of genetic and emotional personality traits upon which the acquired traits are built, their existence and impact is not directly addressed and considered in building theories of entrepreneurship. Internal capital, on the other hand, considers accrued and genetic predispositions as vital and equal in terms of their importance for entrepreneurship. Attributes such as intelligence, imagination, creativity, expressiveness, the ability to conceptualize and abstract, senses (sensing the environment), temperament, physical appearance, birth rights (place/citizenship), and inheritance have been marginalized (in terms of being considerably addressed), primarily because there is very little one can do about them, especially in policy-making.

- Internal capital is considered a "fluid" quality (at least parts of it) and can be disposed of at the control of the individual, while human capital is more conceived as passive in terms of exchanging it with something else. In our notion of internal capital a person can exchange part of his capital with other individuals or entities such as organizations, the market and the physical world. The potential to provide labor, which is also included in internal capital, is one case of exchange for food, money or other valuables. Sharing ingenuity in the form of ideas with others in exchange for their support or contribution is also an exchange in internal capital.

- Human capital is usually conceived as invariant, at least for short time periods, while internal capital is dynamic and differs from one moment to the next, even if that is by the simple act of living/breathing, as energy (physical and mental) needs to be exchanged to sustain one in life.

- Internal capital includes many aspects of social capital as it includes the effect of the entrepreneur's network and social circles. The influence one can exert on others in the form of control over them is leverage at the disposal of the entrepreneur in making things move the way he wants. It belongs to him to use as he pleases.

An important aspect of internal capital that is vital for our interpretation of multipreneurship is the weighing of the various traits it includes from the point of view of importance in the existence and behavior of individuals. Naturally, safety is more important than pleasure (rationally thinking anyway) and so we would expect that activities to ensure one's safety take priority over any higher-order needs such as engaging in entrepreneurship, for example. As another example, it would be unnatural and inefficient (not to mention ineffective) to expect that one would be interested in venture formation when starving.

This brings in focus the notion of the hierarchy of needs that we usually see in theories of developmental psychology. A classic representative of this case is the hierarchy of needs that Maslow developed in 1943. In his scheme, which we will also adopt and extend here, a description of human motivation is outlined in terms of fulfillment of needs in order of their importance for one's survival and growth. Starting from the basic and fundamental needs to the emotional and then to the more conceptual and abstract, the various levels include:

- *Physiological needs:* necessary for the functioning of the human body, such as food, water, air for metabolism, clothing and shelter for protection from the elements and sex for reproduction and sustainment of the species.

- *Safety needs:* from infrequent natural and human events such as natural disasters, social disruptions such as economic crises and various forms of violence and abuse.

- *Social:* involving interpersonal needs such as feelings of belonging, acceptance, intimacy, friendship and love.

- *Cognitive:* including the desire to be accepted and valued by others in social, professional and personal settings. In simple terms, it's the need to make a positive impact on other people's lives. The value of this need can be measured by the self-esteem and self-respect one has for himself.

- *Self-actualization:* is the need to realize one's full potential and accomplish everything that one can.

To the aforementioned list we will add one more need that became evident in Chapter 4 when we presented the case of high-profile/high-level multipreneurs. This goes one more level up and expresses the need for someone to be something beyond what they can:

- *Legacy:* is the need to be remembered as something important and significant to the lives of future generations. Perpetuating in the memory of others in time is an important drive that is not directly addressed by the other needs.

Although as a trigger and motivator of actions, legacy could be considered as part of self-actualization and the cognitive needs, we believe it deserves a separate mention as the motivations behind it are different philosophically since it addresses metaphysical needs. Being accepted by others as a cognitive need could potentially include legacy, but the level of reward and feedback one gets from fulfillment of a cognitive need is directly perceived by the individual, while the notion of legacy, at least from the individual's point of view, is purely a mental dimension that can differ in expression from a cognitive need. In addition, reaching one's full potential is personal and private in essence and has a mark or a point in time beyond which there is nothing more anyone needs or should want to do.

Leaving a legacy is a need that projects the impression that the individual in some sense will perpetuate in time in the minds of others. For example, while a cognitive need might trigger one to donate to charity, a legacy need might drive them to create a fund that will provide ongoing help and support to a cause past and beyond their lifetime. Seeking breakthroughs is another example of legacy need as it addresses the need to go beyond the recognition of the living and extend to the future of an individual. Wanting to be remembered, say like Einstein, Beethoven or Michelangelo, is something that the need for legacy tries to distinctly encapsulate.

Of course, each individual is different from another, has different life experiences and perceptions of themselves and consequently the breadth of each one's needs will vary. In our framework the needs are the parts of the internal capital that drive the flow of thought through the network of the traits and attributes of an entrepreneur while being themselves attributes. Figure 6.9

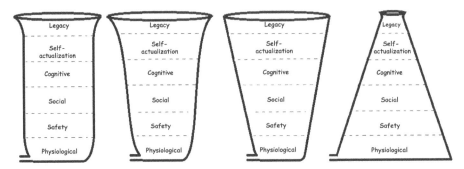

Figure 6.9   **Hierarchy of needs for different individuals**

shows the hierarchy of needs for different individuals as represented by different shapes of containers. The leftmost container is closer to the representation of a hierarchy as most people are familiar with and how Maslow imagined it.

Differences in the social and natural environment one is raised in and functions along with the various influences (see system perspective in Figure 6.3) allow different amounts of needs to be satisfied. The more one is able and the environment provides, the more needs they can fulfill (liquid level in the vessels of Figure 6.10) and the higher they are in the hierarchy. Satisfying needs is not exactly like filling a bucket as we have a constant demand for them and we have to satisfy them from environmental sources. In an analogy with the container of needs, it's more appropriate to imagine the vessel as a container with a hole at the bottom. We need to constantly keep fulfilling our needs if we are to stay alive and rise in the hierarchy. As long as the inflow matches the outflow we can remain in a steady state. If say the economy is not doing well and we lose our job, the inflow will be less than the outflow and our physiological and safety needs will be at risk. If on the other hand our entrepreneurial ventures become successful, the surplus of inflow will raise the level of the liquid in the container and higher-order needs will be satisfied.

Something that is beyond the scope of this book and more in the realm of philosophy is that this hierarchy of needs is not set in stone and for some reason human beings have the amazing capacity to shift them up and down according to certain aspects of them. Take for example the extreme case of a Buddhist monk. His social needs are apparently zero, while his self-actualization needs have been transcended to another level. Similarly, while his physiological needs still remain, the need for safety is not of primal importance to him. This person could very well be an exceptional multipreneur if he wanted to but he is content and happy by his own choice.

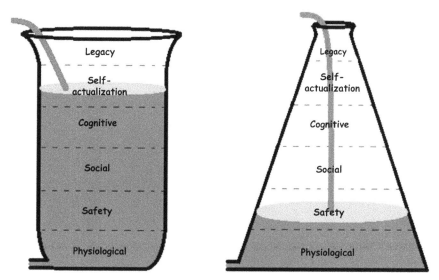

Figure 6.10 **Flow of satisfaction of needs**

Combining the needs with the traits and attributes we mentioned as internal capital we get a more complete picture of what the introduction of this new concept is trying to achieve. Due to lack of a better representation, we will merge the images of Figures 6.8 and 6.10 into what we will call from now on a pictorial representation of internal capital (Figure 6.11). The network nodes should be seen as floating around the various need levels, as the same attribute—such as autonomy for example—can be used in satisfying different types of needs.

The advantage of the representation we chose comes from the ease with which we can introduce entrepreneurship and by extension multipreneurship in a market setting (Figure 6.12). A new definition of entrepreneurship using this representation would include any business activity that contributes to the increase of the internal capital of an individual, through a supply and demand process if we want to include economic terms. The elegance of the new concept is that it allows for other activities to raise the internal capital, such as engaging in and appreciating art, music, sports, etc.

In addition to being able to represent individuals (entrepreneurs, associates, employees and customers) using internal capital in a framework for multipreneurship, we can also abstract other entities such as private organizations (banks, funds, corporations, etc.) and public entities (government, NGOs, associations, etc.). Even nature can in a sense be represented as having

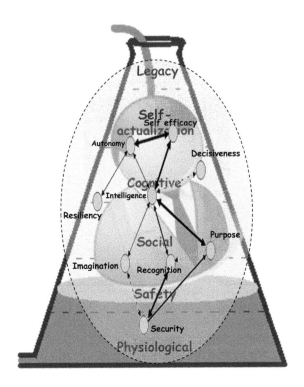

Figure 6.11   Internal capital and networked attributes

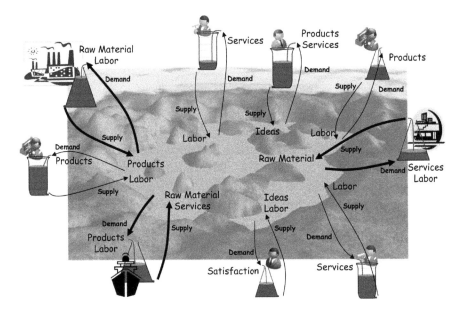

Figure 6.12   Internal capital exchanges in a market setting

internal capital that generously supplies to us, demanding our labor in return (which is not of much use to nature, though). This is an important element for the framework we are presenting here as it allows the interactions amongst entities to be represented with an exchange mechanism based on internal capital units. A market in that sense is nothing more than a virtual representation of an internal capital exchange.

In real life the market is not as visible (water) as the landscape of Figure 6.12 displays but more like the one in Figure 6.13. Visible (water bodies) opportunities get exploited fast so eventually the depth of the water (profit) becomes low, so subsequently one has to work hard to reach out to new water bodies. This takes place in an anomalous terrain, with limited visibility and other competitors searching for the deepest "wells" at the same time. In their search entrepreneurs also want to keep the process as invisible as possible until they've set up the process and exploited the opportunity well before anyone else.

Figure 6.13   The market terrain from the perspective of entrepreneurship

6.3   External Capital and Market Process

Having defined internal capital as more or less everything under the complete control of the entrepreneur, we will define everything else as external capital. This includes nature and everyone else's internal capital (including their impressions of the entrepreneur). To bring this close to the economic approach of explaining behavior, we include in external capital other individuals, social groups, organizations, the government and everything that can interact with the entrepreneur. The market is nothing else in that sense but a place where each individual is exchanging internal capital for external through a supply process and the opposite through a demand process (Figure 6.14). The aim is always to have a net surplus that will increase and fill up their "vessel" with internal capital. In a probably more poetic approach, internal capital is like the juice of life and entrepreneurs are trying to fill their repositories with it.

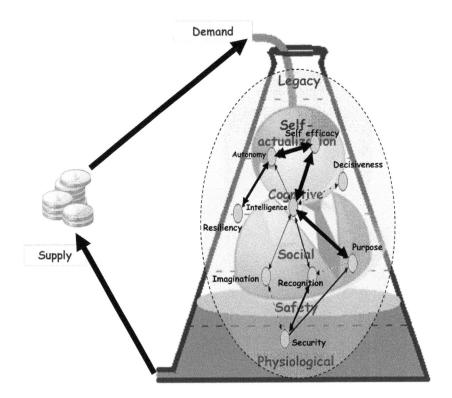

Figure 6.14   **Entrepreneurship through supply and demand of**
                internal capital

The basic interaction in a market according to the definitions we gave is that of an exchange. This is the process by which entities exchange internal capital. The entrepreneur spends some of his internal capital to exploit an opportunity in a market. Other people contribute their internal capital partnering with the entrepreneur to build the venture. Nature or some other entity is enabled by the venture to contribute more capital in the form of products and services. Customers eventually come and consume the capital provided by the contributing agents and in return they selectively give some of their own to the entrepreneur and his team (Figure 6.15).

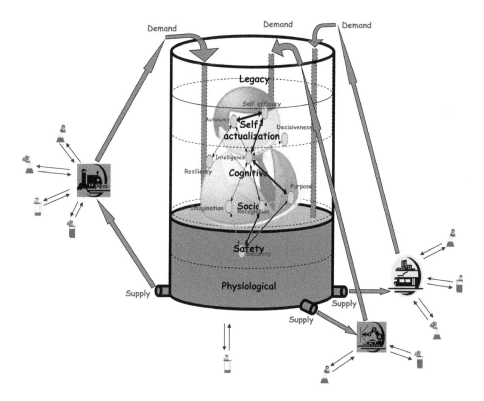

Figure 6.15   Multipreneuring with supply and demand streams

A new definition of entrepreneurship based on the concepts we presented so far will look like: *entrepreneurship is the activity by which a group of entities use their internal capital to enable access to greater amounts of capital for customers in exchange for money.* The greater amounts of capital are usually provided by Mother Nature, even if that is not directly visible, or in the more visible sense from the competition. Cutting shares from an existing business for example is draining the internal capital of that business and brings it in our vessel. The monetary contribution of the customers is also a form of their internal capital that they probably acquired through labor or other means (trade, investments, etc.).

Using an analogy to visualize the entrepreneurship process, it is like building a well to drill water. Many people can join the entrepreneur in building the well. Sometimes the efforts are successful and water fills the well, while other times their efforts go to waste. As soon as water comes up the well, people/customers come and pay (money or labor) to drink. If the area around the well is like a desert and there are few wells or no other wells, a lot of customers will be attracted and the entrepreneur and his team will become wealthy. The downside is that as soon as the success of the well becomes known, others will try to drill nearby to benefit from the internal repositories of the land. This discovery process will eventually drain the well (or lower the quality of the water) and the entrepreneur will have to seek other areas to drill.

The case of multipreneurship is an example of an exchange process that involves exchanges of internal capital for exploitation of many diverse opportunities (Figure 6.15). Having a successful business means a lot of rewards for an entrepreneur in terms of internal capital and include among others a strong feeling of financial safety and job security, increased self-esteem and confidence in his abilities, along with enhanced feelings of control and power. These are all contributions to his internal capital that raise the level of his repositories. This excess of capital can be invested now to pursue another venture (successful presumably) and the process can repeat itself for as long as the entrepreneur has capacity for more internal capital and the environment external. One key point here is the capacity of the environment to provide capital. This, as we said before, is in relation to the capital other individuals and entities can afford and what the physical world of accessible and unexploited resources can provide.

6.4 The Discovery Process

Having defined the constituents of the market that will allow us to explain entrepreneurship, we need now to describe the aspects involved in the entrepreneurship processes and later on in multipreneurship. The first element in developing our framework is to explain how opportunities are discovered and exploited. The structure and behavior of the market will be instrumental in addressing these two issues.

The market landscape, as we mentioned before, is not static and while at times of economic growth it can be susceptible to entrepreneurship, at other times it can be quite restrictive. The landscape of Figure 6.13 displays such differences by analogy of physical landscapes. Entrepreneurs can be seen as explorers in that space continually seeking opportunities. Over that landscape there are paths to successes and paths to failures, all connected in a network of resources, people and any other entity that could influence the formation of firms.

We will adopt the view of the entrepreneur's world as a network of entities (see Chapter 1), some of which he can reach directly, while for others intermediaries need to be involved. In looking for opportunities, individuals need to traverse their network until they locate one opportunity that appears promising. Establishing the shortest possible path to them will be the most efficient way to make it happen, provided of course they, along with their partners, have adequate internal capital to spend for its realization.

Two major ways are provided in mathematics for exploring interconnected network and tree structures. These are the breadth-first and depth-first methods and are displayed in Figures 6.16 and 6.17 respectively. Breadth-first involves traversing concentric circles from where we are and increasing their radius each time we complete one. In network notation this means we first explore the nodes immediately connected to us, then we move to the ones immediately connected to them and we go on until we find what we want or we exhaust the network. This method is advantageous if we are lucky enough to have what we want near us, but it's quite consuming in terms of steps if what we want is far from us.

Depth-first, on the other hand, allows deep searches all the way to the edge of the network then backtracks one node, follows another path to the edge, backtracks and carries on. Eventually all this backtracking will lead back to the starting point, then choose the next closest node and repeat the process. As in the previous method, luck is also important here as what we are looking for might be right next to us and we missed it simply because we are too busy exploring a hint in depth.

In real life both methods are greatly influenced by our knowledge and familiarity with the structure of the network. For this reason we included in Figures 6.16 and 6.17 the circles of influence of the entrepreneur. The bigger and more far-reaching, for example, his family circle is, the faster he can perform a breadth-first search for opportunities and maybe gain a visible picture of his surroundings before venturing deeper and further into his network.

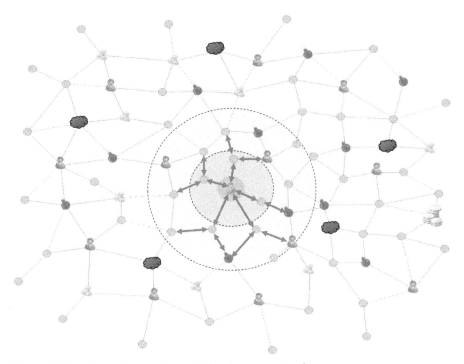

Figure 6.16   Breadth-first search in the opportunity space

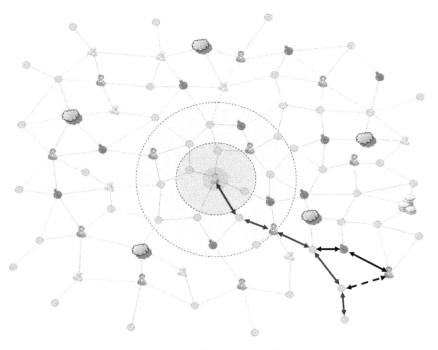

Figure 6.17   Depth-first search in the opportunity space

Interpreting this in another way, it might mean that if one is born in a family that has entrepreneurial roots and traditions, it will be easier for him to search and especially exploit opportunities. Family support in that direction is vital for starting up a business.

A more realistic representation of the discovery process is probably one guided by heuristics and intuition where the entrepreneur's mind drifts in a dream-like way, throughout the opportunity space in his neighborhood and visualizing and imagining sometimes potential opportunities across the space (Figure 6.18). Some of these paths will at times look more rational or interesting, drawing more attention and eventually deem themselves worthy of exploration. At that time a breadth-first process with branches of breadth search along its branch will be adopted to investigate possible alternatives that will lead to the target, eventually taking the shape of an exploitable opportunity (Figure 6.19).

Figure 6.18   Browsing in the opportunity space

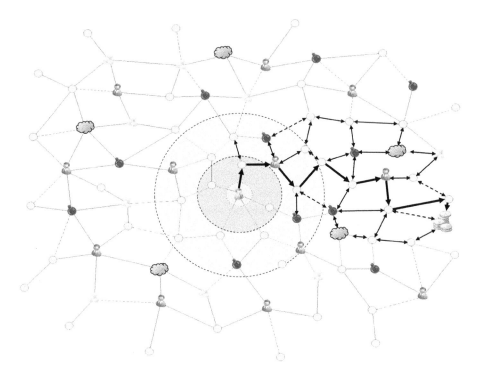

Figure 6.19   Heuristic search in the opportunity space

6.5   The Exploitation Process

Unfortunately the diagrams adopted so far don't do justice to the difficulty involved in the discovery and realization process, as they display the market and the venture process the way an entrepreneur builds it in his mind. A better understanding of the intricacies of the search for opportunities will come by imposing the influence of the terrain/market and its visibility in the search process. Distance impedes visibility as does the morphology of the terrain. Looking at the market space from where the entrepreneur stands, the network will look like the one in Figure 6.20. Entities close to the entrepreneur will look more prominent than the ones further up. In addition, there will be collaborating entities with their perception and representation of the market that will influence the impression the entrepreneur has of the space accordingly.

All anthropomorphic entities including partners, competitors, other organizations and customers are represented now with their internal capital. The network of connections of the entrepreneur with entities and resources is shown with dotted lines simply to indicate it is not yet selected for the

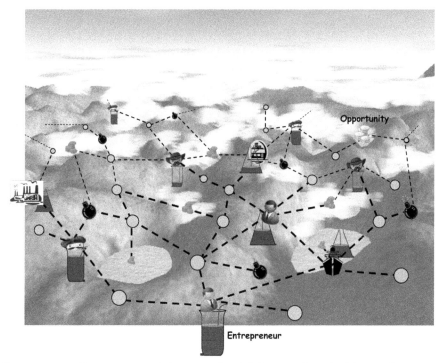

Figure 6.20   Entrepreneurial network with internal capital in market space

exploitation of the opportunity. Failures (bomb icons) and successes (gold icons) are also part of the life of the entrepreneur and are displayed in land or water formation. Some parts of the landscape are clear so one can see potential opportunities that might exist there, while in other cases one has to guess if opportunities exist and where exactly they are. Visible and easily accessible sources of capital are getting explored faster, while more distant ones follow next. A lot of them are partially or completely hidden, requiring more of a guessing and trial and error approach for their discovery and exploitation.

When an opportunity is identified the entrepreneur starts the internal capital exchange process through his various circles of influence and progresses until he reaches his destination (Figure 6.21). Partners and resources will be accessed and recruited along the way, forming the venture and its supporting entities. Eventually a direct line of supply and demand of capital is established, allowing the entrepreneur to experience a net inflow of capital (Figure 6.22).

If we were to see the exploitation process in time it would look like pieces (entities and resources) coming together one after another, forming the firm

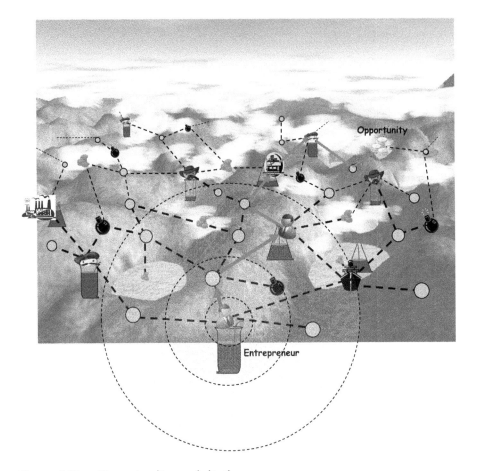

Figure 6.21   Opportunity exploitation

up to the point of the first production and delivery of the product or service the opportunity represented (Figure 6.23). Through the timeline the potential for profit moves up and down as we get closer to the final goal and according to the achievements, missteps and breakthroughs the entrepreneurial team faced and overcame in its path. Recalling the diamond probe we introduced at the beginning of the chapter, the entrepreneurial timeline in Figure 6.23 is a description of "What" takes place (red rectangular parallelepiped), in a time/"When" (horizontal axis) and place/"Where". "Who" refers to the entities involved in the process while "Why" is the past of the entrepreneur that led him to the point in time when the exploitation of the opportunity process began.

Bringing everything together we can summarize the answers to the aspect of the diamond probe of Figure 6.1.

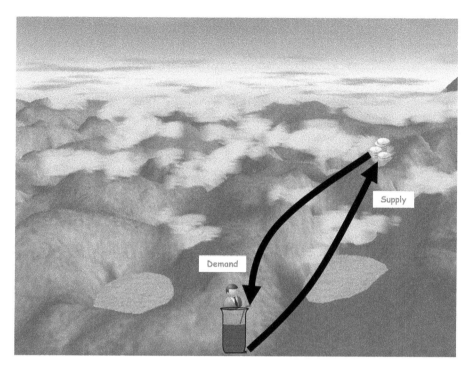

Figure 6.22   Established venture in the form of supply and demand flows

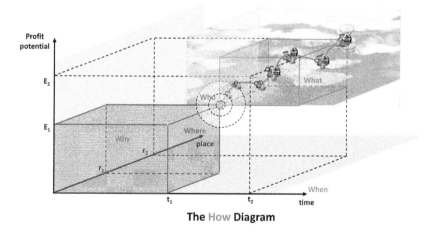

Place: physical and virtual

Potential: dynamic potential of the interaction
amongst entities – something line
entrepreneurship

Place = x,y,z,i (i =0 for imaginary and 1 for real
space)

Figure 6.23   Entrepreneurial firm formation timeline

The aspects each vertex addresses in our case include:

- "When": Entrepreneurs are in constant search for opportunities. Given their availability and market conditions, a potential opportunity will come into focus and become the exploitation target.

- "Where": This is directly linked to "When" and refers to the geographical and virtual places where all action took place.

- "Who": Starting with the entrepreneur who just decided to exploit an opportunity and an initial core of human and physical resources he believes are required for the realization of the venture, we move into time and space materializing the final entrepreneurial team. Customers are virtual in the process and physically attached to the venture as it begins operating in the market.

- "What": While many actions are common, like the build-up of the team, ensuring financial support and dealing with the legal and operational aspects of the new venture, some might be product- or service-specific.

- "How": The decision-making process—everything we mentioned up to now in this chapter.

- "Why": The motivations and rationale behind intentions and actions that lead to decisions. Refer here to the push and pull factors we mentioned in Chapters 3, 4 and 5.

6.6   The Case for Multipreneurship

In order to make the final leap from entrepreneurship to multipreneurship we need to assemble everything we have presented so far and, combining it with the theoretical findings presented in the research literature, build a possible model of multipreneurship. Combining the various concepts we brought together in explaining entrepreneurship, we can extrapolate their features and derive the visualization of multipreneurship of Figure 6.24. As the image shows, we see the exploration and exploitation process that is enabled by the network of qualities, attributes and external entities of entrepreneurs and, through the principles of supply and demand, that allows the exchange of internal capital that leads to a steady surplus for the multipreneur.

The transition to multipreneurship that entrepreneurs of various levels attempt has its roots in both psychological and economic factors and is influenced by the close environment and the networks individuals build. The attraction to diversification seem to be elemental in the personality of multipreneurs and its display as they mature changing from what appeared as a push effect initially to its pure state as a pull effect. The engagement in diversification also implies that multipreneurs have high tolerance in going through the difficulties of setting up a firm and can effectively leverage their past accomplishments.

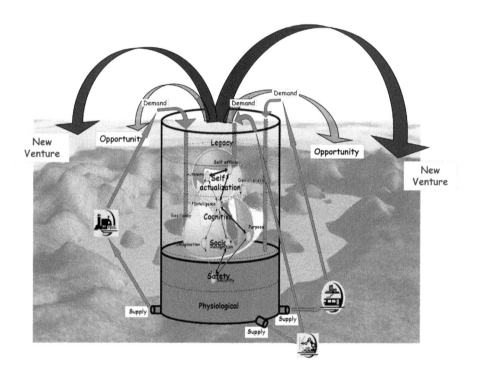

Figure 6.24   Converting opportunities to supply and demand streams

MULTIPRENEURIAL DRIVES

From the presentations in the previous chapters one could easily identify three drivers that cover more or less the growth initiatives in every case of multipreneurship: *security*, *fulfillment* and *excitement*. Security is evident in low-level multipreneurs and essentially, in their case, diversification aims at sustaining one's income during fluctuations of the micro business environment. In the same way as a restaurant with a single item on the menu has lower chances of success, an entrepreneur focusing on one type of business is solely dependent on the behavior of the market segment his product or service targets. Staying focused on one industry exposes an entrepreneur to competition from existing and new entrants, changing customer needs and preferences and the political, social and economic environment that influences that market. Low-level multipreneurship is dominant in many poor countries around the world and in economies with high unemployment rates. Although in these cases multipreneurship is triggered by the need to ensure survival more than anything else, one cannot ignore the growth and excitement factors at least in their more basic forms.

At the higher level of entrepreneurship, although growing through diversification might count as an attempt to secure one's welfare level and fortune (an indication of mature entrepreneurs), the drive for fulfillment is dominant. Multipreneurs and conglomerate organizations are drawn by a vision to reach the highest levels of existence in the business world. They achieve this by forming strong entities that cross national boundaries and cultures. Forming a business empire is similar in drive to the expansion tendencies of the great historical empires. It's just the field that happens to be a different one. The market as the terrain of business and economic activity has a different nature than the geographic terrain the old empires were seeking to expand. The terrain is now shaped by consumers and its hills and valleys represent their capabilities to buy and consume.

Fulfillment comes from a sense of destiny and it appears to be prevalent in high-profile multipreneurs, tracing in many cases a generation back. It brings a sense of continuity between the past, present and future and acts as a primal drive pushing multipreneurs ahead. It is clearly reflected in the aspirations and spirit of their family and the lessons and inspiration they got from their parents. It gives them the satisfaction that they performed their duty, the origin of which can be traced to their parents and role models of their childhood and early adulthood.

Excitement, on the other hand, is expressed in two ways in their level. One category includes the excitement for creating a new business, while the other refers to the excitement of producing a certain product or service (a case for technology entrepreneurs). Creating a new business is like any form of creation that is naturally satisfying in itself. Rewards are easy to see and feel;

they engage other people and they expand the physical and emotional space. Creating a product or service, though, where none existed before is a different feeling and involves the excitement of the discoverer and pioneer. This is a primal kind of excitement, purely emotional and levitating and involves the thrill of adventure and exploration.

MULTIPRENEURIAL SKILLS

A typical question that arises at least in academic research is whether repeat entrepreneurial performance is due to innate talent or the accumulation of entrepreneurial experience. This apparently is in relation to market context rather than anything else as the more one is engaging in a particular market, the more experience one acquires and the easier it will be to deal with familiar problems specific to the nature of the particular market. In our case of multipreneurs, though, the market specifics are of little influence since the individuals we study venture in diverse markets and so one would expect that a different element needs to be involved. The primary candidate for that role is talent. The question is, talent in what?

Looking at the skills that successful multipreneurs have might provide part of the answer. Skills that are considered essential include, among others, the ability to network with other individuals, financial and government establishments, an understanding of how organizations function and perform and a great sense of the generic market mechanisms with the consumers and their communities. Other skills, such as understanding financial statements and negotiating deals, might also be essential.

Of great importance is the fit between the business venture and personality of the multipreneur. It is evident from their backgrounds and styles that their business ideas seem to match their personalities. For example, if we were to read the childhood and early adulthood of the high-profile multipreneurs we presented in Chapter 4 and then be presented with a list of business types, chances are extremely high that we would match multipreneurs with their real businesses correctly. Although this might sound obvious here, in real life mismatches are a major source of failures. This proves the point that knowing who you are and going after the things you like are vital for success in life.

An entrepreneurial skill that occasionally shows up in literature and that one would expect to see in multipreneurs is empathy. As part of emotional intelligence, empathy is a characteristic that great leaders display; high-profile multipreneurs are, in many respects, great leaders, so one would naturally expect that they will be high on empathy. This is also expected primarily because the sense of knowing the customer and providing accordingly is often expressed through an understanding of the customer's position as human beings with needs and wants. While this does exist in multipreneurs and is expressed especially during a firm's genesis, it is later expressed more on an intellectual or market-driven level rather than on the personal level that has been theorized to exist. It is true that entrepreneurs build things and provide services that satisfy the needs of people, but this is purely on the basis of receiving a return in exchange, which is something that generally people with high empathy do not expect.

An undeniable skill for multipreneurs is their expertise in executing their plans. Multipreneurs tend to be exceptional executioners and in that respect they are excellent project managers. The main difference from them is the personal stand they take towards risk, as a project manager tends to be on the risk-adverse side of things. Firm formation always involves risk and multipreneurs seem to feel quite comfortable taking risks. While normal entrepreneurs seem to have gone through the risk-taking phase and settled after their firm reached maturity, multipreneurs are comfortable with (even "drawn to" at times) risk and view it as a natural part of the business formation process. Risk is higher at the start-up level and reduces as a firm reaches maturity. The type of risk is also different during the various stages of firm growth. At the beginning and in the aftermath of the exploration phase, the entrepreneurial team is young and the venture idea is not crystallized yet, resulting in an internal/organizational form of risk that team dynamics create. Later on, when the firm reaches maturity, the nature of the risk becomes more external as organization performance is more affected by the social and market environment in which it operates. Multipreneurs are quite comfortable with the crisis management type of risk and as such they outperform others in the first category of risk at the start-up phase. This enables them to engage in diverse ventures again and again. For the second/external type of risk they seem to delegate control to subordinates who they leave in charge of their established firms and intervene only in the face of crisis.

A side effect of risk-taking that is often ignored by theorists and practitioners, especially those involved in policy-making, is the high probability of failure (brown arrows in Figure 6.24). By their own nature, multipreneurs engage in diverge ventures that involve different industries and as such it's like starting from the beginning, at least with respect to learning the specifics of an industry. One can easily see that running an airline is different from running a restaurant or developing a microwave. Multipreneurs are bound to fail, but this certainty appears normal to them and they see it in a completely different light—learning. Of course, as a child perfectly knows by instinct, failing is the only way to learn how to walk, and in that sense falling is not a failure but part of learning how to stand up. Multipreneurs seem to have retained that aspect of learning and they are quite tolerant to failure.

THE MODEL

Combining the skill arsenal we described before and fueled by their motivation drivers, multipreneurs engage in their primary activities, opportunity identification and risk-taking. Intuition and a calculative methodology are their allies in the process. The rewards from risk are the success factors and the return on their investment as it is the factor that breaks stagnation and affords the possibility of going higher. As such it carries with it the probability of going lower and eventually leading to failure. This is where multipreneurs excel by managing to engage their support network and dissipate the risk across their connections. The difference, though, from the average entrepreneur is that they don't really do that in an attempt to minimize risk on themselves, but mainly to ensure it is minimized with respect to the endeavor. For that reason they make sure they have the support of a strong and committed team as well as place an unparalleled value on execution. Strong teams for multipreneurs are more like strong alliances that are respected and valued. As such, multipreneurs are not afraid to share their earnings with those that helped them build their empires, whether they are team members, other businessmen, politicians or supporters. In doing so they ensure their future support, an investment they will cash in on in the form of success in new ventures.

Having ensured the successful flow of profit from one enterprise, multipreneurs turn their attention in search for new opportunities. If they discover promising ones, they engage in forming new ventures to exploit them. Some of them will fail, but some will be successful and become part of the profile of the multipreneur. At this stage, as we saw in the previous chapters, the multipreneur effectively closes to his benefit the circle of supply and demand that related to the opportunity (Figure 6.25). The situation will repeat itself for as long as the "glass of self-actualization" has room to fill and lifetime doesn't run out.

Internally we can say there is a conversion process, where the benefits of the effective supply and demand circles of the established business are converted to new business streams. Some of them will succeed and in this way will be converted to efficient supply and demand circles, while others will

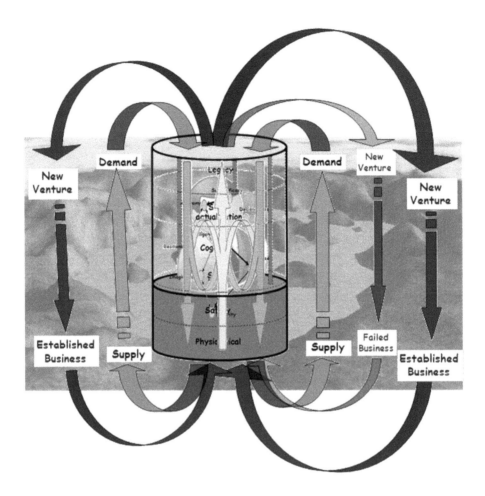

Figure 6.25   Multipreneurship model

fail, weakening the established supply and demand cycles. The advantage of multipreneurs is that they can convert failure into learning that strengthens their internal network of skills and attributes and can be used to raise the probability of success in future opportunity exploitation cycles. While this representation also explains serial and the general category of portfolio entrepreneurs, we can add a special feature in the case of multipreneurs, which is their unique ability for breadth experience/capacity that, combined with their ability to delegate depth to the right experts, allows them to reach the diversification levels we observe.

Chapter 7
Scaling Up and Out

Entrepreneurship and, by extension, multipreneurship have the capacity to raise economies in ways that do not have to result in the destruction of others. Having more people express entrepreneurial potential is an issue of scaling up the phenomenon and increasing the supply of entrepreneurs. We have two choices to follow in that direction: scale up and/or scale out. Scaling-up is a multiplicative approach that implies a central control (like government). This is the most natural way of doing it, as the primary enabler of it, the state, has the resources to support such functions. Scaling-out, on the other hand, implies a more distributed approach, where one replicates a process through multiple approaches and in different situations.

Diversifying in businesses has been seen as one of the ways to grow in a protective way that minimizes the impact of the volatility that individual industries can experience. Following such a strategy is displayed at the extremes of the entrepreneurship spectrum, which includes the low-level (solo) entrepreneurs and the high-profile (billionaire level mainly) entrepreneurs. One can naturally wonder if the conditions at those ends allow for the display of such behavior or if there is something inherent in these individuals that drives them to diversify. Multipreneurship sometimes seems like an attention deficit disorder that cannot keep entrepreneurs in one area, kind of like the artist who experiments with different media.

Interestingly, though, multipreneurial behavior is also displayed by organizations, especially when they form conglomerates. The ultimate form of multipreneuring still is expressed by governments of any form and level, as they have to address the needs of the diverse sectors for the societies they serve. Separating individuals from organizations and governments might seem artificial, since organizations and governments are led by individuals, but it is being done in this book to address the collective nature of decision-making in organizations that leads to multipreneurial behavior. In that sense one would expect different drivers and traits to be involved as well as different types of interaction that trigger and sustain such behavior.

To scale entrepreneurial behavior we need to consider the growth stages of individuals as they are born, grow, become professionals and turn to entrepreneurship. The model (Figure 7.1) we considered in the previous chapters in this respect includes certain genetic characteristics that predispose someone to aggressively seek societal challenges, a family environment that is supportive of independence and creativity while instilling discipline and effectiveness, and a society in need of entrepreneurial displays. Bringing these elements together, we have the birth of entrepreneurs. With critical and efficient exploitation of opportunities, these entrepreneurs mature and break through the ceiling of success in their venture to multipreneuring by engaging in venture formation in different industries. Driven by the need to leave a legacy behind them, most multipreneurs will become philanthropists in the later stages of their lives.

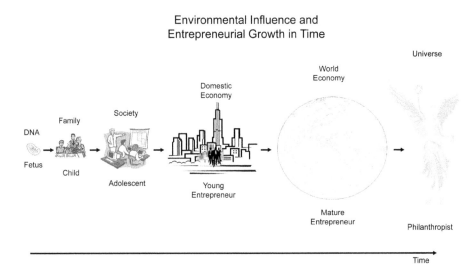

Figure 7.1   **Environmental influences and entrepreneurial growth over time**

With the exception of the first stage in Figure 7.1, in which there is very little one can do (unless in the future we find the "entrepreneurship" gene that we can trigger to express the behavior), all other stages present opportunities for influencing the entrepreneurial predisposition individuals might have. In the early stage of the family environment, the potential entrepreneur can only be indirectly influenced by exposing primarily the family providers to entrepreneurship so they in return can infuse some of the attitudes required for future display of entrepreneurship.

Until a child with entrepreneurial potential gets out in society, there is very little direct intervention we can do to encourage and train the young in entrepreneurship. From the moment children engage in primary, secondary and, later on, tertiary education, societies through their representatives, the government and local authorities can start influencing entrepreneurial predisposition. While these stages are vital for cultivating entrepreneurship in students, we will not address them here as our primary focus is on multipreneurship. This defaults any scaling efforts to the levels past the first entrepreneurial initiatives and into the realm of mature entrepreneurs.

Considering general attributes, probably the most influential characteristic one could identify in entrepreneurs that dominates by magnification to multipreneurs is their risk-taking ability. Risk-taking has an inherent limitation that prevents most individuals from following through or even attempting to engage in start-up formation, and that is the probability of failure. Uncertainty is ingrained and is at the core of risk-taking, meaning that unanticipated and unaccounted circumstances are bound to often lead to failure. Tolerance for failure is a necessary ingredient and part of life for successful multipreneurs. Having experienced failure and gained valuable lessons from it, successful multipreneurs in general tend to appear humble, at least in their public profiles. Even when occasionally they might show the opposite (usually in displays of power), one can definitely see in them the kind of shyness that wisdom brings.

A critical aspect we need to always keep in mind and a stand this book is making is that disposition towards entrepreneurship (or the elements one can break down from it) is to an extent a personality trait that some people have and others do not, regardless of the effort we occasionally make to present it as an acquired trait. Much like height is an asset when playing professional basketball, some multipreneurial traits, such as open-mindedness (necessary for diversification), either exist in someone (at least at a minimum) or they do not. So while we will be talking about things to do, one needs to keep in mind that we are referring to those individuals that are born with the minimum "design" elements that can support multipreneurial behavior.

Whichever way we choose to promote multipreneurial behavior, we have to make sure the *drivers*, the *skills* (genetic capabilities and acquired) and *conditions* are there in their right proportions to enable the behavior to surface. Unfortunately each one of these elements are controlled and influenced in their majority by different actors. Drivers have to do with upbringing and in that sense are instilled by the close and early environment of an individual. Family or its substitute in this case is the lead influencer, so if we are to do something here we can only hope to educate parents on the benefits of instilling strong drivers in their children and by promoting appropriate role models that can motivate individuals. Inspiration will act as the spark of drive that can light the entrepreneurship fire in someone. A strong driver in the direction of multipreneurship is openness to new ideas and concepts, something that can be easily achieved through education, for both parents and children. A renaissance-style approach to humanities and social sciences can greatly complement other fields such as science and engineering at the school and high school levels.

The skills category is more adept to interventions since many can be acquired through training and education. Business skills can certainly be taught to a great extent and can be acquired by working in businesses. Additionally analytical skills, such as basic mathematics and domain knowledge, can also be acquired through education and experience. On the other hand, there are other types of skills that are mostly a matter of talent. Being outgoing, open-minded, intuitive and insightful — although greatly enhanced with proper mentoring — are primarily an issue of temperament and genetic predisposition more than anything else. Being forthcoming and able to network is also another category where talent rules despite the notion promoted by many educational institutions (for marketing purposes mainly) that it can be taught.

The last ingredient for encouraging multipreneurial behavior is the type of economic and market conditions that can nurture the seed of entrepreneurship and enable it to flourish and grow. This category is totally under "our" control (under rational conditions at least) and can be affected by proper laws and measures that governments and policy-makers can initiate to stimulate entrepreneurship that will eventually lead to multipreneurship. Tolerance for failure is probably the most desired condition as it will encourage the risk-taking attitudes needed to explore volatile market conditions. These are the environments that entrepreneurs usually take advantage of and their efforts will eventually lead to the creation and growth of strong enterprises.

Scaling-out refers to expanding it into social groups that haven't yet displayed strong multipreneurial behavior, such as students, women, immigrants (this is debatable), scientists, engineers, artists, public and civil servants, to name a few, into market mediums and modes such as online commerce, low-level entrepreneurship, serial entrepreneurs, etc. Due to the size limitations of the book we will only cover generic ways and mediums and leave it up to the reader to expand to other segments and categories as they please. Further information can also be found in the supporting bibliography of this book.

7.1   The Online Dimension

The Internet was probably one of the most profound life changes in modern times and has reached the levels and spread that affords anyone a chance to engage in social activities. Unfortunately, building a network and finding the right intermediary that will eventually connect an entrepreneur with consumers is much more "random" than ever, simply because the scale of the available options "fogs" individual entities, making it difficult for quality products and services to distinguish themselves. For example, let's assume this book is a quality publication (hopefully) and let's say that in order to promote this book we reach out to experts who could endorse it. Let's say that the real and well-known experts in the field of multipreneurship were about 50 and that 5 of them (10%) are positively inclined at that time to endorsing a book. Let's also assume that in the past these experts would receive 10 such requests per year and would probably accommodate one of them (10%). These numbers are small enough to allow them to browse through the books' details and read and endorse the one that would interest them the most.

Nowadays, in addition to the field of expertise being widened (on the Internet anyone can claim to be an expert), the same experts would receive 100 such requests, making it impossible for them to go through all of them even if they wanted to. Let's assume for convenience purposes that from 50, the experts online appear to be 500 (and this is underestimating reality—one only needs to check the publications, directory and social media entries for entrepreneurship to see how this number can be reached and even exceeded). Let's also assume the same percentage (10%) of them as positively inclined to endorsing a book. Actually, the real experts are probably overwhelmed already and the percentage of them who are willing to endorse a book is much less, but for the sake of the argument here and to counter potential other errors in the calculations, we will keep this percentage the same. The chances of this book being endorsed by a real expert that could boost its sales 10- or even 100-fold dropped from $(5/50)*(1/5)$, or 2%, before the Internet to $(5/500)*(1/5)$, or 0.2%, after the Internet.

What this percentage shows is the pollution effect of the Internet and the randomness it has inflicted on promoting quality. Of course one could argue that the customer base has been widened (although regarding certain items such as this book, this is more of a myth than a reality). At least in the case of books similar to this one, which are mainly library acquisitions, the market has changed very little, so one should expect to sell more now than before. While this is true in general, what is not taken into consideration is that with

Figure 7.2   The Internet globe

the expansion more blurring appears, similar to when more atmosphere interferes with our vision when we look in the distance, making it more difficult to see clearly (not to mention it allows mirages to appear).

The Internet has made everything look like a convexly curved landscape (such as the surface of a hollow earth with us facing the inside of this huge sphere rather than then outside), covered with webpages and where everyone has a telescope (Figure 7.3). You can see everything as far as you want, but your field of vision is extremely narrow and at times it is affected by atmospheric conditions (Internet garbage). Now try to imagine that you are sitting on this world and want to draw attention to something you wrote on a page. You start waiving your hand, yelling, flashing lights and even jump up and down to draw attention. How many people do you think will see your signal and turn their telescopes to your page even if somehow they know that in your location (say California) there is a sage like you?

In reality the Internet added a lot of randomness while enhancing the rewards. Something like a lottery, where a few win a lot and many lose a little. The few that get noticed seem to experience an explosion of attention like a chain reaction. This is a dynamic situation so the momentum can shift quickly to other sources unless the "fire"/content is fed continually to keep the interest strong. Eventually what happens is mediocrity gets promoted more than real expertise. Depth has been replaced by breadth and everything comes and goes so fast that websites rise and fall in their millions.

For every successful venture on the Internet there are many others that never reach their full potential. Successful ventures such as Facebook, for example, caught up primarily because they targeted an initial well-identified following that was easy to access. Facebook was built to bring together students and alumni of Harvard University and ended up being the top social network site in the world. The initial critical mass was easy for them to achieve as the communities they targeted (Harvard and later the greater Boston area) were extremely susceptible to the idea it was supporting, giving the company the initial boost, shining more like a lighthouse rather than a flashlight to use our analogy of Figure 7.2.

With the world of social media full blown, the business world has experienced a slew of new practices ranging from new marketing strategies, financing options and even new products that never existed before. Google is probably the ultimate example of a modern product/service that only concerns information. As a case in point, Google probably has the simplest homepage ever built but it allowed the company to deliver exactly what people needed and nothing more. In doing so they became the top-most Internet company in the world. The momentum of the online world also changed the profile of entrepreneurs we were used to seeing and gave rise to a new breed of entrepreneurs who traditionally were not associated with business. Although in the past (and especially in the case of multipreneurs) we would see unconventional founders with interdisciplinary experience, nowadays we see huge numbers of younger recruits from diverse backgrounds breaking out from all sectors. The Internet enables anyone with motivation and skills, to play an active role in shaping their future instead of passively waiting for an economic cure that governments could provide. As the speed of social change continues to accelerate, it will create additional opportunities and the trend to invent and engage in business online will grow stronger to respond to growth, eventually raising economic and living (hopefully) standards globally.

7.2   Female Multipreneurship

As we saw in the chapter on low-level multipreneurs, women in poorer regions of the world engage in entrepreneurship frequently (conditions permitting—such as raising a family). This might be driven by the realities of life in these regions, requiring both parents in a family to work to supplement their income and make do, but nevertheless entrepreneurship is expressed and contributes greatly to their local economies. Multipreneurship for them is as vital as for men and the main driver remains that of security through diversification.

At the higher end, though, while we observe some entrepreneurial activity (still lagging significantly behind men), we see an almost non-existent presence in multipreneurship compared with their male counterparts. This is also reflected in academic research as female entrepreneurship is a particularly understudied group. That doesn't necessarily mean there is a lack of capabilities on the part of women but rather an environment not quite supportive of such behavior, at least at the multipreneurship level.

Women in many societies are subjected to a conditioning from early on in their life and this later on leads to the stereotypical preconceptions that they are either not interested in business, or they are not capable of rising to the levels men achieved. To comment on this type of popular belief we must first remove from the analysis those groups of women who are deprived of such opportunities due to physiological and social traditions that limit them in engaging in entrepreneurship. Physiological factors usually include giving birth, raising children and engaging in strenuous physical activity, while tradition can include social and religious expectations that limit the role of the women to carrying out household responsibilities.

Having removed these "natural" and imposed cultural limitations and considering equal access to resources and opportunities, we might find that it will then become an issue of confidence and competence. Both sexes might confuse male displays of confidence as signs of competence, which naturally might lead to the belief that women are not good enough to be promoted as leaders more than men. Displays of confidence are frequently adopted by men as remnants of archetypal power displays in establishing territory and ensuring submission. This is also supported by the established fact that leaderless groups show a natural tendency to elect self-centered, overconfident and narcissistic individuals as leaders. These personality characteristics are apparently not equally common in men and women. When there is lack of skill competence, one relies upon appearances and in that field confidence will always lead.

Paradoxically, though, the skill set one needs to be a successful leader includes competencies to a much greater extent than confidence, making the previous trend to promote confident individuals to leadership positions counterproductive. This is in reality the primary cause of leader failure. Considering the reversal that we just presented, we should expect women to perform better (equally, at worst) as leaders than men. This notion is also supported by research that finds women more likely to elicit respect and pride from their followers. Apparently, women seem to communicate their vision effectively, they are willing to share the spotlight of success and they allow more expressiveness in their subordinates while empowering and mentoring them. If all these characteristic sound familiar, it is because they represent the maternal characteristics usually attributed to women. Interestingly, these facts are also characteristics of transformational leaders.

Female entrepreneurship and, by extension, multipreneurship is an underutilized resource that is only recently beginning to draw attention and gain momentum. A way to grow the impact of women entrepreneurs and encourage more to join the field is by developing support networks that can help and mentor newcomers and by promoting appropriate role models who can influence and inspire women to become entrepreneurs. Only then will we be able to see how they can expand into the multipreneurship field. Education and training will also help in raising the appropriate skill levels, but its role should be more of building and changing women's perceptions of themselves as entrepreneurs than anything else. Considering everything from that perspective and assuming necessary societal changes, we should expect women to be great entrepreneurs and by extension successful multipreneurs (at least comparable in numbers with men).

7.3 Ethnic Multipreneurship

The growth of ethnic populations in Western societies brought with it a wave of entrepreneurial activity by immigrants. Targeting both the ethnic and host communities, ethnic entrepreneurs have an easy entrance and support (at least at the start-up phase) from the market segment of their ethnic group. Further growth, though, will be dependent on their interaction and the opportunities offered by the host community. While the term ethnic entrepreneur usually refers to minorities formed by immigrants entering a host society and building businesses, we will also consider here pre-existing minorities such as the Native Americans in the US and the Roma in European countries. The extent of engagement of these communities in multipreneurial activities is mainly with respect to low-level multipreneurship. From the literature point of view, studies regarding their engagement at the higher end of multipreneurship are almost non-existent, so in our case here we will just mention general facts and trends about ethnic entrepreneurs that might help one deduce the potential future these individuals might have as multipreneurs.

Business activity from minorities is nothing new and has always existed in some form or other in most societies. In recent times, waves of immigrants that strongly influenced and allowed the build-up of minority "islands" within host societies was enabled by certain circumstances. The major wave of immigrants came from former colonies, southern Europe and North Africa and was enabled by the demand for labor and the economic restructuring of the Western markets that shifted from working in large firms to self-employment in smaller ones. This eventually led to the resurgence of small and medium-sized enterprises.

There are many theories that attempt to explain the observed entrepreneurial preferences of immigrants over employment in host firms. The main propositions attribute immigrant entrepreneurship to the fact that by default immigrants were the more entrepreneurial members in their country of origin that saw migration as an opportunity for exploitation. In simple terms, it is assumed that entrepreneurial predisposition was the drive for immigration and as such it will also be preferentially expressed in the host communities. Another well-established proposition is that external factors in the host environment, such as discrimination or entry barriers to the local labor force due to language deficits and education, push immigrants to self-employment. A mix of both probably lies at the heart of this complex phenomenon, especially now that we see immigrant engagement moving away from the stereotypical traditional corner shop to diversified sectors such as information technology, leisure and recreation, global trade and real estate, to mention a few.

Apart from the drivers, opportunity structures and group resources play an important role in the development of ethnic businesses. Opportunities created by an ethnic group are distinct and usually can only be addressed by members of the group. Starting a business to address their needs enables a preferential treatment for the start-up, ensuring its support from the minority consumers. Types of immigrant business that target both host and ethnic communities have an even better chance of survival as they have the steady pool of their ethnic community, while also cutting market shares from the host community. These advantages can only work for the initial phases but for talented multipreneurs might provide the break they need to expand and grow into high-profile multipreneurs.

Tapping into the potential of ethnic pools might be a way for governments and policy-makers to stimulate economic growth. At the high-profile end of the multipreneurship spectrum, as we saw from some of the cases we presented, many multipreneurs were immigrants that grew their businesses in host communities. At the higher level it is also imperative for multipreneurs to reach out beyond the national boundaries of their first ventures, if they are to continue growing, and in that sense they are immigrants (of higher status of course) in the countries in which they expand. At this high level there is nothing much one can do to encourage multipreneurial behavior, as the multipreneurs themselves probably know better than anyone else how to do it.

Factors that might help multipreneurial behavior of ethnic entrepreneurs include low entry barriers in terms of required capital and educational qualifications, allowances and support of small-scale production. Additional factors include high labor intensity and low added value. This might not be so desirable, though, from the social welfare point of view, as it usually triggers cut-throat competitions. Forcing self-employment as a way of absorption and economic mobility might encourage entrepreneurship, but it's unlikely that will have an impact on multipreneurship simply because of the different drivers that enable the latter.

7.4   Social Multipreneurship

Social entrepreneurship (SE) refers to the formation of enterprises whose purpose is to solve a pressing and insurmountable social problem. The concept usually addresses three types of organizational form: for-profit SE, hybrid SE and NGOs (non-government organizations). The first category is of interest to us in this chapter in terms of multipreneurship primarily because the other forms have already been discussed in Chapter 5. The interesting characteristic of the for-profit SE is that it is a means to an end instead of an end in and of itself. Profit in this case will enable the enterprise to address a social need or solve a societal problem. Such aims will eventually raise the living standards of societies and allow their communities to prosper.

The motivation behind such altruistic endeavors is the empathic nature of individuals and is enhanced by the belief that individuals can contribute and influence societal change as well as the state. The characteristics one needs to possess are the same as those of traditional entrepreneurs and by definition include a creative personality that is imbued with enthusiasm, curiosity and wide interests, coupled with tolerance for complexity and ambiguity. Harmonious passion (not obsessive) is also a strong ingredient and it brings with it a lot of qualities such as love and joy for the self-defining activity one chooses to engage in. Being that they are strong believers in society's capabilities, we need to add to the mix of their personality traits the propensity to cooperate, trust, social networking, and the belief that people can change and they can affect the world in beneficial ways.

The process of the formation of social enterprises starts with the individual who initiates and manages the start-up creation process. Because of the shift of the focus from profit to the effective solution of a social problem, social entrepreneurs' priority is in establishing an enabling and empowering environment that will attract others with similar perspectives to contribute. They achieve that by engaging their own social networks and building new ones from the bottom–up. These networks then operate in coherence, providing opportunities for social coordination that eventually leads to the emergence of the structured social enterprise. In doing so they change the properties of the social system by modifying the propensity for cooperation and establishing trust, which builds social capital that can be exchanged for contributions and services. In other words, what social entrepreneurs do is empower society to pursue and realize change.

While elements of social entrepreneurial activities exist in many firms along with their commercial activities, in our case we will focus on pure social entrepreneurship entities and we will let the reader's intuition fill in the intermediate spectrum. Geographically speaking the phenomenon of social entrepreneurship is widespread, but according to Global Entrepreneurship Monitor varies tremendously across countries, from 0.2% to 7.6% of the adult population. In general, though, regions with higher pure commercial activity (such as the Caribbean, Sub-Saharan Africa and Latin America) also exhibit comparatively higher rates of pure social entrepreneurial activity. Several interesting findings about social entrepreneurs include the high prevalence of women, their young age and their diverse educational and work backgrounds.

Because of the nature of the social enterprises in terms of their vision and mission, one expects to find striking differences from normal enterprises and other social activities. While this is true, a major difference is the strategy of social activities where the focus is in solving a social issue with social activism going head on for change, whereas social entrepreneurship aims at facilitating a long-term process that will provide a sustainable solution to a social issue. It is kind of a philanthropy move with the twist of engaging people in the solution instead of providing top–down solutions. In this way it is far more superior to social activism because affected people do not need to remain passive receivers of support but instead they become part of the solution. In doing so, they build their personality and skills and become capable of replicating the creative process elsewhere. It's an enabling process aimed at building capable individuals who can change or at least make the world a better place.

Enhancing the role social entrepreneurs play and creating more of them can be supported by outsourcing social activities to individuals and non-profit organizations by the state and by helping through educating primarily the young in acquiring social consciousness. Developing compassionate and self-aware individuals and instilling community engagement is something the state can do, either in educational settings or by providing appropriate incentives. Multipreneurship in the field would then be observed because the rewards will fuel social multipreneurial behavior.

7.5 The Role of Education

Multipreneurship education does not have meaning without addressing the first step, which is entrepreneurship education. The latter has always had a bit of an identity crisis, as it usually conjures visions of intelligent tinkerers creating technology gadgets and risking all in the pursuit of personal and financial glory. Setting the picture straight requires a lot of effort and involves governments, policy-makers, reactionaries and educators. A list of skills one needs to become an entrepreneur that need to be presented and learned include the ability to identify opportunities, project management techniques, handling tax and legal issues, communication principles, management of networks and the supply chain, and so forth. In essence and apart from domain knowledge, these skills include all the practical skills one needs to function in the real world.

One of the ways people learn is through education and training. Introducing entrepreneurial objectives in the curriculum can enlighten students and inspire them to explore their entrepreneurial tendencies in a formal way. Teaching entrepreneurship and experimenting is schools and university settings with business simulations could be one of the many methods one can use to support the behavior. This is more vital for sciences and engineering than social sciences and humanities where students are exposed to economic and human elements of societies and the world. The importance of engaging hard sciences students in entrepreneurship is vital, as we are living in a world shaped by technology and where progress is usually associated with research and industrial development in fields that never existed before, such as nanotechnology, biotechnology, media and communications, to name a few.

At the higher education level a lot of the skills required for entrepreneurship can be addressed through the general education curriculum that the liberal arts institutions follow in the US and through specialized design courses that bridge business with technology and other areas with entrepreneurial potential. Providing support for start-ups, either directly through government and state funding or through venture capital, is the next phase one can tie to education. A good example is the US case where the market is probably the most susceptible in the world for expressing entrepreneurial behavior. In fact, if other countries could provide to their citizens the opportunities available to US entrepreneurs, we would have probably experienced an inflation of entrepreneurial growth similar to that of the big-bang. This type of development will more likely result in an evolutionary scale-up for human beings.

Fundamental concepts of entrepreneurship can be tailored to the curriculum and complement academic programs. The practical element of converting technological innovation into market products can be introduced in selected courses or as dedicated modules to entrepreneurship where students will be exposed to the concepts and processes of effective business practices. Start-up formation should be simulated and promoted to inspire prospective scientists and engineers in seeking application of new products and services and engaging in entrepreneurial ventures to exploit their innovations. Even if one is not going to be engaged as an entrepreneur, the knowledge and understanding of the particulars of business will greatly contribute to their understanding of organizations and the processes they adopt in developing, manufacturing and distributing products and services.

Setting up business incubators (Figure 7.3) where students can learn more and experiment with the organizational and business aspects of a start-up can be valuable in preparing future entrepreneurs for a successful career in business. Access to such environments from financial institutions and venture capitalists will allow for early adoption of promising ideas and provide the financial support an incubating entrepreneur needs. These incubators are not meant to provide just training, but their primary purpose would be to act as networking platforms where future entrepreneurs can find potential similar-minded partners and collaborators. Potential entrepreneurs need to learn to break national barriers and allow prospective entrepreneurs to communicate across the globe and form partnerships with similar-minded individuals who complement their skills and can join them in exploiting opportunities.

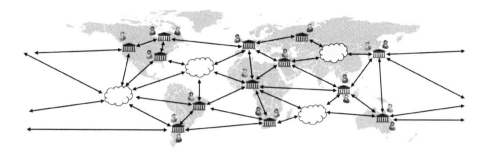

Figure 7.3   Networking educators and future multipreneurs

If the initiatives are successful and increase the supply of entrepreneurs, one can easily expect that a lot of them will cross to multipreneurship.

7.6   The Role of Policies

Governments are primary influencers in markets despite the capitalist doctrine that wants them as regulators. The very simple fact that governments are social entities means they are affected and are affecting the social networks that societies form and entrepreneurs exploit. As actors in the world economy, governments shape the market space by the measures they take to support their economies. Given the advantages and value entrepreneurs add to their environments and their communities, it is natural for governments to want to invest and increase the supply of these visionaries in their economies. In that direction governments usually attempt to establish policies and support institutions in their mission.

As good judgment is instrumental for entrepreneurial success, improving the quality of judgment in a population might be a first attempt at increasing the supply of entrepreneurs. Although this is greatly dependent on someone's genetic predisposition and upbringing, providing the appropriate education at the lower levels can greatly help in this direction. The popular notion that entrepreneurs are optimists shaped by adversity is only supported by anecdotal evidence and cannot form the basis for policies that would support those attitudes, not to mention that incurring hardship might be very difficult for citizens to accept from their elected governments.

In considering the entrepreneur as an individual entity, policies need to adapt to the fact that entrepreneurs are a diverse group with respect to their profiles of human capital and perceptions of themselves and their environment that ultimately affect their motivations and impacts their performance. Gender, age, tradition, ethnic origin, political status and field of expertise can be some of the factors that create the non-homogeneous group of entrepreneurs. Measuring the impact of policies is extremely difficult and often the adopted metrics fail to reflect reality. The increase in the number of businesses, for example, is many times used mistakenly to measure entrepreneurship in an economy. This creates the illusion that more new business means more new entrepreneurs in the market but fails to account for the fact that many new businesses are the result of habitual entrepreneurs and that a lot of them are built with short-term goals of exploiting specific opportunities of temporal and thus limited extent. Additionally, an inherent difficulty always involves the case of incubating entrepreneurs, as it is difficult to account for their numbers and the real trigger behind their transformation into novices. A more thorough analysis of the business formation of the market might reveal the areas where emphasis needs to be placed and the support that newcomers in the field of entrepreneurship need to sustain themselves and grow. The government's role needs to be much more than that of a provider of education and training to boost entrepreneurship. Establishing hotbeds such as Silicon Valley can also be a significant if not vital aspect in raising the entrepreneurial potential of individuals. In this way governments will show that they are not only facilitators of innovation and economic growth, but they are also active participants and creators of that growth.

Scaling up and scaling out systems of innovation is vital for spreading the entrepreneurial spirit. Knowledge and innovation need structures to diffuse across systems, whether in sectors, regions or nations. The primary structure to achieve this is a dynamic network of different actors, such as incubators in state, educational and private settings, firms and financial support providers along with education and policy-makers. Entrepreneurial centers in firms, government and non-government public entities can be part of a system that networks entrepreneurs with human, social and financial capital.

The role of each actor can vary and change over time, but their commitment to contribute should remain steady and continuous. Using the wrong actors or placing them in the wrong place or at the wrong time is bound to create errors and diminish the effect of the network. For example, when scientific or engineering breakthrough is the target, it is unnatural to expect a lot of participation of venture capitalists, so the government's role should be dominant in such endeavors. Supporting entrepreneurship by local governments and the state should also be a reciprocal initiative and the entrepreneurs ought to give back in their local economies by supporting and providing for the local workforce in spite of the fact that a more competitive situation might exist elsewhere. This is quite a dilemma as one might act against the other. Entrepreneurship by definition involves profit maximization, but we argue here that in itself this is not the kind of quality that adds to the lived experiences of individuals.

When forming policies and practices that will support entrepreneurs, one also needs to consider that by its own nature entrepreneurial activity is high risk and often will naturally end in failure. In such cases (productive churn) the entrepreneur shouldn't be penalized in any way that inflicts on his self-esteem and lowers his potential for entrepreneurship. "Failure" is probably the stronger educational practice as it forces individuals to identify the causes behind it and, to the extent that these causes were the result of the entrepreneur's thinking and behavior, they can serve as motivations for modifying behavior to improve entrepreneurial skills.

Although attempts in this direction have been made by governments (such as the Enterprise Act of 2002 by the British government), where bankruptcy laws were adapted to allow for fast recovery, the benefits from the specific practices remain unclear. It is to be expected that governments will always prefer to use public resources in more predictable ways that will increase their visibility in the eyes of voters. In addition to that there is research that supports the notion that individuals do not always learn from their failures because of their tendency to attribute success to themselves and failure to external effects, prohibiting constructive self-criticism and inhibiting learning. Unfortunately, it is difficult to evaluate and predict the judgment quality of individuals who aspire to become entrepreneurs, so encouraging people with poor judgment to make risky decisions will waste resources that could benefit other aspects of the support a government can provide. A side effect of failure is its impact on the entrepreneur's perceptions, as it might naturally trigger the feeling of grief.

All these aspects of failure need to be considered by policy-makers, as overcoming the loss and learning from failure needs to be supported if the entrepreneur is to re-engage constructively in new ventures. Theoretically it is almost certain that a creative person that is properly supported and learns from failure will eventually eliminate all sources of error and succeed. This type of intelligent failure can be a learning experience and part of the education and training process where policy-makers and governments can greatly contribute, especially when multipreneurship is sought.

The case of multipreneurs is even more important for governments because of the breadth of business ventures that can cover diverse spectrums of activity that can enrich communities with diversity and resilience to economic fluctuations. This fundamental contribution to the process of wealth creation can spill over to the rest of society by generating employment and tax revenues that would be missed otherwise. Supporting multipreneurs shouldn't be to the detriment of novices as they represent the primary pool of future multipreneurs, so investing in their growth can result in a tremendous return on investment.

A final note we need to make regarding multipreneurship (and to an extent entrepreneurship): based on the notion that multipreneurs will surface no matter what—and sometimes in the most harsh economic environments—should one leave things as they are? The main question we are actually trying to answer in this respect is whether policy-makers and practitioners should provide assistance to potential multipreneurs. The definite answer here is that, given the successful track record of someone who qualifies as a multipreneur, supporting them in the early stages of diversifying is probably a good idea. One should be careful, though, in the latter stages when they might have reached their cognitive and emotional limits of handling diversity. Another reason for restraining help in the latter stages is that they should have built enough capital by themselves to support their future diversification, so overall it's best to leave them alone to do what they can. They are the experts in their own field anyway, so they know better than anyone else how to find the optimal way to exploit an opportunity. If we were to advise policy-makers regarding novice entrepreneurs, it would again be to ease entry into the field but avoid financial support unless the aim is to fight unemployment.

Bibliography

Almeida, H.V. and Wolfenzon, D. (2006). A theory of pyramidal ownership and family business groups. *The Journal of Finance*, 61(6), 2637–80.

Audretsch, D.B., Falck, O. and Heblich, S. (2011). *Handbook of Research on Innovation and Entrepreneurship*. Cheltenham: Edward Elgar Publishing.

Bosma, N., De Wit, G. and Carree, M. (2005). Modelling entrepreneurship: unifying the equilibrium and entry/exit approach. *Small Business Economics*, 25(1), 35–48.

Branson, S.R. (2011). *Losing My Virginity*. London: Random House.

Brown, F.W. and Reilly, M.D. (2009). The Myers-Briggs type indicator and transformational leadership. *Journal of Management Development*, 28(10), 916–32.

Byers, T., Dorf, R. and Nelson, A. (2010). *Technology Ventures: From Idea to Enterprise*. Columbus, OH: McGraw-Hill Education.

Carter, S., Tagg, S. and Dimitratos, P. (2004). Beyond portfolio entrepreneurship: multiple income sources in small firms. *Entrepreneurship & Regional Development*, 16(6), 481–99.

Casson, M., Yeung, B. and Basu, A. (2008). *The Oxford Handbook of Entrepreneurship*. Oxford: Oxford Handbooks Online.

Chuanming, C. and Junhua, S. (2008). Entrepreneurs' demographic characteristics and their diversified strategic options. *Management World*, 5, 015.

Clark, P., Kays, A., Zandniapour, L., Montoya, E.S. and Doyle, K. (1999). *Microenterprise and the Poor: Findings from the Self-employment Learning Project Five Year Study of Microentrepreneurs*. Washington, DC: The Aspen Institute.

Eesley, C.E. and Roberts, E.B. (2012). Are you experienced or are you talented? When does innate talent versus experience explain entrepreneurial performance? *Strategic Entrepreneurship Journal*, 6(3), 207–19.

Elfring, T. (2006). *Corporate Entrepreneurship and Venturing*. New York: Springer.

Ferrante, F. (2005). Revealing entrepreneurial talent. *Small Business Economics*, 25(2), 159–74.

Forbat, J. (2007). *Entrepreneurship: The Seeds of Success*. Petersfield: Harriman House Limited.

Hagel, J., Brown, J.S. and Davison, L. (2010). *The Power of Pull: How Small Moves, Smartly Made, Can Set Big Things in Motion*. New York: Basic Books.

Halkias, D. (2011). *Female Immigrant Entrepreneurs: The Economic and Social Impact of a Global Phenomenon*. Farnham: Gower Publishing, Ltd.

Harkiolakis, N., Halkias, D. and Abadir, S. (2012). *E-Negotiations: Networking and Cross-cultural Business Transactions*. Farnham: Gower Publishing, Ltd.

Hogan, R., Johnson, J.A. and Briggs, S.R. (1997). *Handbook of Personality Psychology*. Oxford: Elsevier.

Hyytinen, A. and Ilmakunnas, P. (2007). What distinguishes a serial entrepreneur? *Industrial and Corporate Change*, 16(5), 793–821.

Iacobucci, D., Dago, P.M. and Rosa, P. (2004). Habitual entrepreneurs, entrepreneurial team development and business group formation. *Paper presented at "RENT XVIII–Managing Complexity and Change in SMEs"*, 24, 26.

Isaacson, W. (2011). *Steve Jobs*. New York: Simon and Schuster.

Jianjun, Z. and Hongwei, L. (2007). Entrepreneur backgrounds, diversification, and firm performance. *Nankai Business Review*, 5, 004.

Kacou, E. (2010). *Entrepreneurial Solutions for Prosperity in BoP Markets: Strategies for Business and Economic Transformation*. Upper Saddle River, NJ: Pearson Prentice Hall.

Klyver, K. and Evald, M.R. (2012). *Entrepreneurship in Theory and Practice: Paradoxes in Play*. Cheltenham: Edward Elgar Publishing.

Landström, H. (2007). *Pioneers in Entrepreneurship and Small Business Research*. Berlin: Springer.

Leitao, J. and Baptista, R. (2009). *Public Policies for Fostering Entrepreneurship: A European Perspective*. Berlin: Springer.

Lerner, J. and Schoar, A. (2010). *International Differences in Entrepreneurship*. Chicago: University of Chicago Press.

Lundström, A. and Stevenson, L.A. (2006). *Entrepreneurship Policy: Theory and Practice*. Berlin: Springer.

Lynch, P. (1998). Female microentrepreneurs in the host family sector: key motivations and socio-economic variables. *International Journal of Hospitality Management*, 17(3), 319–42.

Miettinen, A. and Donckels, R. (eds) (1998). *Entrepreneurship and SME Research: On its Way to the Next Millennium*. Aldershot: Ashgate Publishing.

Morrish, S. (2009). Portfolio entrepreneurs: an effectuation approach to multiple venture development. *Journal of Research in Marketing and Entrepreneurship*, 11(1), 32–48.

Parsons, J. (1994). *Portfolio Entrepreneurs: Growth and Diversification*. M.Sc. dissertation. Stirling: Stirling University.

Penrose, E. (1955). Limits to the growth and size of firms. *American Economic Review*, 45, 531.

Praszkier, R. and Nowak, A. (2011). *Social Entrepreneurship: Theory and Practice*. Cambridge: Cambridge University Press.

Prügl, E. and Tinker, I. (1997). Microentrepreneurs and homeworkers: convergent categories. *World Development*, 25(9), 1471–82.

Resnick, M. (2007). All I really need to know (about creative thinking) I learned (by studying how children learn) in kindergarten. In: *Proceedings of the 6th ACM SIGCHI Conference on Creativity & Cognition*. New York: ACM, pp. 1–6.

Richardson, G.A. (1960). *Information and Investment: A Study in the Working of the CompetitiveEconomy* (revised edition, ed. D. Teece, 1990). Oxford: Oxford University Press.

Rosa, P. and Scott, M. (1997). Portfolio entrepreneurs: some empirical evidence on the multiple ownership or control of SMEs, and its implication for our understanding of start-up and growth. In: Miettinen, A. and Donckels, R. (eds) *Entrepreneurship and SME Research: On its Way to the Next Millennium*. Aldershot: Ashgate.

Rosa, P. and Scott, M. (1999). Entrepreneurial diversification, business-cluster formation, and growth. *Environment and Planning C: Government and Policy*, 17(5), 527–47.

Rutten, M.A.F. (1991). *Capitalist Entrepreneurs and Economic Diversification: Social Profile of Large Farmers and Rural Industrialists in Central Gujarat, India*. University of Amsterdam: PhD dissertation.

Sarasvathy, S.D., Menon, A.R. and Kuechle, G. (2013). Failing firms and successful entrepreneurs: serial entrepreneurship as a temporal portfolio. *Small Business Economics*, 40(2), 417–34.

Solymossy, E. (2005). Entrepreneurship in extreme environments: building an expanded model. *The International Entrepreneurship and Management Journal*, 1(4), 501–18.

Tihula, S. and Huovinen, J. (2010). Incidence of teams in the firms owned by serial, portfolio and first-time entrepreneurs. *International Entrepreneurship and Management Journal*, 6(3), 249–60.

Tinker, I. (1995). The human economy of microentrepreneurs. In: Dignard, L. and Havet, J. (eds), *Women in Micro- and Small-Scale Enterprise Development*. Boulder, CO: Westview Press, pp. 25–39.

Ucbasaran, A.D. (2004). *Business Ownership Experience, Entrepreneurial Behaviour and Performance: Novice, Habitual, Serial and Portfolio Entrepreneurs.* Nottingham: University of Nottingham. Retrieved from http://etheses. nottingham.ac.uk/380/ (accessed 14 February 2014).

Ucbasaran, D., Alsos, G.A., Westhead, P. and Wright, M. (2008). Habitual entrepreneurs. *Foundations and Trends in Entrepreneurship*, 4(4), 309–450.

Ucbasaran, D., Westhead, P. and Wright, M. (2001). The focus of entrepreneurial research: contextual and process issues. *Entrepreneurship Theory and Practice*, 25(4), 57–80.

Ucbasaran, D., Westhead, P. and Wright, M. (2006). *Habitual Entrepreneurs.* Cheltenham: Edward Elgar Publishing.

Ucbasaran, D., Westhead, P. and Wright, M. (2009). The extent and nature of opportunity identification by experienced entrepreneurs. *Journal of Business Venturing*, 24(2), 99–115.

Ucbasaran, D., Westhead, P., Wright, M. and Binks, M. (2003). Does entrepreneurial experience influence opportunity identification? *The Journal of Private Equity*, 7(1), 7–14.

Westall, A., Ramsden, P. and Foley, J. (2000). *Micro-entrepreneurs: Creating Enterprising Communities.* London: Institute for Public Policy Research.

Westhead, P., Ucbasaran, D. and Wright, M. (2003). Differences between private firms owned by novice, serial and portfolio entrepreneurs: implications for policy makers and practitioners. *Regional Studies*, 37(2), 187–200.

Westhead, P., Ucbasaran, D. and Wright, M. (2005a). Decisions, actions, and performance: do novice, serial, and portfolio entrepreneurs differ? *Journal of Small Business Management*, 43(4), 393–417.

Westhead, P., Ucbasaran, D. and Wright, M. (2005b). Experience and cognition do novice, serial and portfolio entrepreneurs differ? *International Small Business Journal*, 23(1), 72–98.

Westhead, P., Ucbasaran, D. and Wright, M. (2009). Information search and opportunity identification: the importance of prior business ownership experience. *International Small Business Journal*, 27(6), 659–80.

Westhead, P., Ucbasaran, D., Wright, M. and Binks, M. (2004). Streams of experience and performance: novice, serial and portfolio entrepreneurs. *IGA Zeitschrift für Klein-und Mittelunternehmen*, 9(1), 1–14.

Westhead, P., Ucbasaran, D., Wright, M. and Binks, M. (2005a). Novice, serial and portfolio entrepreneur behaviour and contributions. *Small Business Economics*, 25(2), 109–32.

Westhead, P., Ucbasaran, D., Wright, M. and Binks, M. (2005b). Policy toward novice, serial and portfolio entrepreneurs. *Environment and Planning C: Government and Policy*, 22(6), 779–98.

Westhead, P. and Wright, M. (1998). Novice, portfolio, and serial founders: are they different? *Journal of Business Venturing*, 13(3), 173–204.

Wiklund, J. and Shepherd, D.A. (2008). Portfolio entrepreneurship: habitual and novice founders, new entry, and mode of organizing. *Entrepreneurship Theory and Practice*, 32(4), 701–25.

Wright, M., Robbie, K. and Ennew, C. (1997a). Serial entrepreneurs. *British Journal of Management*, 8(3), 251–68.

Wright, M., Robbie, K. and Ennew, C. (1997b). Venture capitalists and serial entrepreneurs. *Journal of Business Venturing*, 12(3), 227–49.

Index

Note: page number in *italic* type refer to Figures.

For Product Safety Concerns and Information please contact our EU
representative GPSR@taylorandfrancis.com
Taylor & Francis Verlag GmbH, Kaufingerstraße 24, 80331 München, Germany

www.ingramcontent.com/pod-product-compliance
Ingram Content Group UK Ltd.
Pitfield, Milton Keynes, MK11 3LW, UK
UKHW051832180425
457613UK00022B/1211